OLDEN TIMES REVISITED

Olden Times Revisited

W. L. Clayton's Pen Pictures

By Washington Lafayette Clayton

MINROSE GWIN

Editor

University Press of Mississippi / *Jackson*

Publication of this book was made possible in part
by a grant from the
University of Tennessee Better English Fund,
established by
John C. Hodges.

Library of Congress Cataloging in Publication Data

Clayton, W. L. (Washington Lafayette), 1836–1921.
  Olden times revisited.

  Articles originally published in the Journal,
Tupelo, Miss., May 5, 1905–Dec. 14, 1906.
  Includes index.
    1. Southern States—History—1775–1865—Sources.
  2. Southern States—History—1865–1877—Sources.
  3. Frontier and pioneer life—Southern States—
Sources. 4. Clayton, W. L. (Washington Lafayette),
1836–1921. I. Gwin, Minrose. II. Tupelo journal
(1876) III. Title.
F213.C633 1982   975.03   81-21919
                                          AACR2
ISBN: 978-1-60473-880-3

Contents

Preface

In my preparation of this collection, I am indebted to many different individuals in many different ways. I particularly wish to thank my professors at the University of Tennessee who believed in this project and who supported and advised me when I needed help. In the English Department, Professors Joseph B. Trahern, Bain T. Stewart, Robert Drake, and Jon Manchip White gave me valuable practical advice and substantial doses of encouragement at various stages in this endeavor. I am especially grateful to Professor Michael A. Lofaro for reading about half of the original *Pen Pictures* and for giving me many helpful suggestions about editing them. In the Journalism Department, Professor Kelly Leiter helped me with my research of Mississippi newspapers of the period.

I wish also to thank the trustees of the University of Tennessee Better English Fund, established by John C. Hodges, both for the publication subsidy which helped make this book possible and for a travel grant which allowed me to make a trip to the Mississippi Department of Archives and History in Jackson to conduct research for this project.

I am grateful as well to Mississippians Anna Keirsey and George McLean, David Baker, Doyce Deas, and Ann Abadie—all of whom have been enthusiastic and helpful. I am particularly indebted to Dorothy Abbott for presenting the first pieces of this manuscript to the University Press of Mississippi. I would also like to acknowledge the valuable critical suggestions given to me by Seetha Srinivasan, editor of the University Press of Mississippi, and by the reader of this manuscript. The staffs of the Lee County Public Library in Tupelo and the Mississippi Department of Archives and History have been most helpful.

My greatest debts are to members of my own family, and it is to them that I dedicate this volume:

To *Stewart Philip Clayton Sr.*, who preserved the *Pen Pictures;*
To *Erin Clayton Pitner,* who insisted upon their importance;
To *Louis Gwin,* whose help amounted to collaboration;
To *Carol,* who endured.

OLDEN TIMES REVISITED

Introduction

THESE COLLECTED ARTICLES, originally published from May 5, 1905, through December 14, 1906, in the small struggling *Journal* of Tupelo, Mississippi, are Washington Lafayette Clayton's first-hand reminiscences of life in the frontier and Civil War South. In the three-quarters of a century since they were originally published, the sketches have been used frequently by historians of the period 1840 through 1875; yet, to us today, their value adds up to more than the sum of historical fact. Clayton's "Pen Pictures of the Olden Time" are rare, delicately etched portraits of history which stop life in its traces, conveying a sense not just of how things *were,* but of how they actually felt to the nineteenth century Southerner who lived through them. More than that, Clayton's "Pen Pictures" present questions about the ambiguous nature of the South—the paradox of its heroic vision and bitter reality which still haunts historians and literary artists. Although in these reminiscences Clayton looks back to the past—often with a deep sense of loss—he is in one sense a forerunner in his probing insistence to get *at* the South, to dig to its core, to define its illusiveness. In this sense, "Pen Pictures of the Olden Time" may be viewed as a quest for the meaning of the Southern past, rather than a mere remembering of it. Though Clayton calls the "old scenes . . . philosophy teaching by example," they provide for us now, perhaps as they provided for Clayton's readers so many years ago, tantalizing clues to the enigma of Southern history.

Above all, Clayton's "Pen Pictures" give us a sense of what it meant to be a Southerner before, during, and after the Civil War. Almost invariably, he writes of his own experiences—as a boy in frontier Mississippi where "scorpions" lived in trees and wolves roamed hungrily; as a young Confederate soldier bewildered by the senseless destruction of Sherman's march; as a self-taught, circuit-riding lawyer whose fascination with law and with the people he met on the trail flavors many of these stories and sketches. Clayton's work is valuable for many reasons, but its appeal lies in its immediacy. These are *his* experiences, his friends, his war, his defeat—his life in retrospect.

Clayton was both typical and atypical of his world and time. In the events of his life and in his response to those events, he was like many men of the hill regions of Mississippi, Alabama, and west and middle Tennessee. Born in 1836 at Clayton's Grove in northern Alabama, he came to Itawamba County, Mississippi, when he was four years old and grew up in a frontier region only recently vacated by the Chickasaw nation—an environment which provided material for his lush descriptions of the beauties of unblemished nature. One of several children in a struggling frontier family, young Clayton worked at odd jobs and attended a male academy until he was eighteen. In the "Pen Pictures" he recounts wryly his early struggles to make ends meet, his difficulty in finding a job as a subscription school teacher when he was "a boy then, less than twenty . . . and wore a fuzzy quilled cap . . . rather large for my head." With no formal training in the law but "having read a little in Blackstone," Clayton was admitted to the bar in Fulton, Mississippi, in 1858—more from the largess of older lawyer friends, he admits, than through any skill or learning of his own. He married Mary Agnes Bell in 1860, but upon hearing the summons of "the war tocsin," parted almost immediately from his tearful bride to fight for his beloved "Lost Cause." He served in the Civil War with the rank of captain. Because he was frequently called upon to command his regiment and because elevated military titles in accordance with social status were customary, he was given the honorary title of "colonel," by which he was known through his life. He died in 1921.

Certainly Clayton's life followed much the same course as that of many of his peers. He was a man of his times who was moved by the events and emotions which motivated many white Southerners during the period of 1840–1875 and who held many of the same values: family, honor, courtesy, community. Although he was awarded personal and professional honors throughout his life, it is through his writing that Clayton the lawyer-soldier-historian distinguishes himself. At the age of sixty-nine he began writing a 1200–1500 word column which would run weekly for twenty months on the front page of the *Journal.* Judging from the prominent position of the "Pen Pictures" in the *Journal*—usually front page center—and the length of time the columns ran, Clayton seems to have had a loyal readership. The popularity of the columns may also be inferred by Clayton's style of writing directly to his readers, particularly to the "old timers"; by his use of particularities which would interest local people; and by his own pragmatic approach to the articles: "I desire to say, readers, that unless I thought these 'Pen Pictures' were read by many with interest, I surely would not go to the trouble and labor to prepare them."

In describing his preparation of the "Pen Pictures," Clayton makes no pretense of having kept records of the events he describes: "I write also wholly from memory, having kept no diary of transactions in these olden times." It was a meticulous memory, however, which provided material for these articles. Clayton is careful about—even obsessed by—dates, places, proper names. His reminiscences about the Civil War and his experiences as a soldier are as accurate as they are vivid. Clayton joined the Confederate Army in 1861 as a captain of cavalry and served throughout most of the war in armies operating in west Tennessee and northeast Mississippi. His last major campaign of the war found him trailing Sherman on the devastating march to the sea through Georgia; and the war ended for Clayton in April 1865, just a few days after Lee's surrender to Grant at Appomattox Court House, Virginia. While much of his writing about the war is devoted to personal glimpses of the conflict through a soldier's eyes, his recall of dates, names, and troop movements matches accurately with historical works published both before and after his reminiscences.

Yet, while the "Pen Pictures" are certainly factual on the whole, their historicity is partly limited by Clayton's own philosophy that history is "philosophy teaching by example," portrayed for the purpose of bringing "one more ray of sunshine to flow into the life of those with whom we associate." Like Benjamin Franklin, Clayton believed strongly that an individual life should be morally instructive to posterity. He is often unwilling to discuss—except in oblique terms—any distasteful qualities of the people of the "olden times." His reminiscences thus contain colorful descriptions of good deeds, humorous incidents, clever legal manipulations or business wrangling, crafty policing—yet there is a marked lack of villains and villainy in "Pen Pictures of the Olden Time." Even when Clayton must say something derogatory about a person, he often does it so obliquely that only an insider would know of that person's evil deed or character flaw. Also, in rare cases when he must present distasteful information about a person, he often does so in a sympathetic manner. Obviously, this one-sidedness in his character sketches also is largely due to the fact that Clayton was not writing fiction: often his characters were alive, or if they were dead, their memories were being cherished by their relatives. It is to Clayton's credit, however, that working under these external and self-imposed constraints, he still manages to imbue his descriptions of persons of the "olden times" with a startling clarity and with a sweeping sense of movement and life. Again, it is Clayton's eye for detail that brings the characters of his "Pen Pictures" to life: the circuit clerk who carries all office papers in his hat, the abysmally silent Dr. Moore on his bony horse, the stutterer "Uncle Dick" who "sang as glibly as any bird and prayed as eloquently as any minister."

More important than the factuality of the "Pen Pictures" is their ability to impart to us today an emotional perception of the past. Clayton's reminiscences are deeply personal. As such they encourage us to respond to them on a personal level by enveloping ourselves in history and savoring the personal flavor of the "olden time" remembered. Clayton thereby invites us to a somewhat complex response to history: his is not a "you were there" kind of writing, but rather he gently beckons us to look back with him to a time long gone and to pretend, for the moment at least, that we too remember it.

Underlying Clayton's personal memories are both national and regional concerns of the turn of the century. His sense of loss associated with the country's disappearing frontier and his ideals of an instinctive harmony between man and nature place the "Pen Pictures" in the mainstream of American thought and literary development. At the same time, the sketches are peculiarly Southern in Clayton's deeply felt sense of community, his insistence upon a chivalric code of behavior, and his elevation of the past as an example of the values of honor, dedication to country, and harmonious living.

More than any other theme, Clayton's preoccupation with the Southern past provides a unifying thread through the "Pen Pictures." The articles are, above all, reminiscences not only of a past, but of a way of life irrevocably lost. At its core, of course, was slavery. Clayton's view of that institution is typically that of the white Southerner of his time. His idealized version of the carefree existence of the slave is in stark, almost ludicrous, contrast to the drudgery and brutality related in the slave narratives. Yet, taken in the context of the "Pen Pictures" as a whole, his statements about the lot of slaves seem, if not accurate, at least sincere representations of what he saw with a vision limited by time—and perhaps also by wishful thinking.

Clayton's ambivalent concept of the enslaved black as both child and property evolves in his Reconstruction pieces into the less complex emotions of fear and resentment at the new-found power of freed blacks. Yet, this resentment seems more directed toward white Northerners than toward the freed blacks themselves. In fact, he shows great indignation at the scams used by crafty "scoundrels" to obtain money from illiterate blacks during this period. Yet, like most white Southerners of his time, he is embittered by the blacks' political power during Reconstruction and mourns the loss of the slave aristocracy. But while Clayton's "Pen Pictures" often embody much of the white Southerner's blindness to the plight of the black both before and after the Civil War, his writing is valuable in that it also embodies the white Southerner's conviction that he was right: the fact that he wasn't does not cancel out the earnestness of that conviction.

The Reconstruction period culminates Clayton's "Pen Pictures" as originally published. In the original articles Clayton often writes about things as they occur to him, making the chronological sequence of his reminiscences difficult to follow. I have loosely arranged the articles, by chronology of events remembered, into five chapters: Clayton's boyhood in frontier Mississippi in the 1840s; his early adulthood as student, teacher, and apprentice lawyer, 1855–1859; his professional associations and friendships throughout his adult life, 1859–1870; his Civil War experiences in several states, 1861–1865; his observations of the aftermath of war in Mississippi, 1865–1875. This arrangement serves to unify the "Pen Pictures" into a coherent whole and to clarify the chronological sequence of events in the articles. The order of the original articles in the *Journal* does fall roughly into this lineal pattern.

To prevent modern readers from becoming bogged down in the many details that Clayton presents, I have also omitted parts of articles which I felt would sorely try readers' patience. I have completely omitted some of the articles for the same reason. In a few instances, I have combined two articles into one when the subject matter is closely related, a combination which is indicated by more than one date on the edited article. Since Clayton is at his best when he is depicting action or assessing character through action, very little has been deleted from articles in the chapters dealing with the Civil War and the characterizations of friends and acquaintances.

Since Clayton does much of his own explaining, I have attempted to keep my notes to a minimum. The propensity of notes in the Civil War section is needed, I think, because Clayton rightly assumed a knowledge of events, places, and persons associated with the war that his original readers possessed and that we, three quarters of a century later, do not. Mississippians interested in genealogy may find the notes identifying individuals and the index helpful.

In all, I have tried in editing these reminiscences to retain their essence and spirit while at the same time considering what part of them provides insightful, entertaining reading for us today. The joy of "Pen Pictures of the Olden Time" is that they are not just for historians or literary scholars: they are for all of us who wish to pretend to remember and thereby to become, if only in memory, part of a past which has molded the present with a far deeper imprint than we may realize.

Minrose Clayton Gwin

CHAPTER I

"Scorpions" and Stagecoaches

THE SOUTHERN FRONTIER
OF THE 1840S

*That beautiful rolling landscape is now a thick mat
of undergrowth, with all of its pastime beauty
and loveliness gone.*

*AS CLAYTON RECALLS the scenes of his childhood in this first
chapter of "Pen Pictures of the Olden Time," his concerns are those
which infuse all of this collection. He finds a compelling beauty and
joy in the past and seems to feel a compulsion to recreate that past in
memory. There is a sense here, as there is throughout all of these
articles, that if the past can be conveyed in precisely the right language, that the reader will be drawn into it and actually experience
it. Clayton strains toward the perfect "pen picture" which would
mystically transport us as modern Connecticut Yankees to his
Camelot of the Southern frontier. His descriptions of the Mississippi
wilderness of the 1840s and its natural wonders are both visionary
and particular. Again, it is the specificity of these descriptions which
makes us "see" Clayton's exotic "paraquites and scorpions," the
"vast forests," the deer "roaming over the hills." Also in this chapter
are precise, colorful descriptions of both the joys of frontier life—its
corn shuckings, fire huntings, and deeply felt sense of community—*

and the perils of the "olden time"—the lack of medical care and resultant deaths; the inadequate stagecoaches and "stage sickness"; the drunkenness and liquor traffic in "groceries"; for run-away slaves, the packs of "nigger hounds" and the owner's lash.

This first chapter about Clayton's boyhood, then, draws us into a contemplation of the Southern frontier, in all of its various particularity, with all of its "fairy tale" romance. This chapter is thus an apt beginning for our gradual immersion into Clayton's real past, and below it, to the deeper soundings of these "Pen Pictures"—the mythic Southern past.

May 5, 1905

In thinking over the scenes that have occurred during my life, I sometimes believe if anyone can cause even but one more ray of sunshine to flow into the life of those with whom we associate, it is his duty to do so, even though it cost him much labor and pains. The old scenes through which an old man has passed ought to be philosophy teaching by example. All have noticed with what eagerness people read anything with which they have had, or now have, any connection. Especially is this true if the incidents related are about the old times and old men and women, some of whom still remain, or who have descendants still living who have access to the writing. Thinking over this has impressed me with the thought that some "Pen-Pictures of the Olden Time" might not be uninteresting reading.

There may be some few older citizens in this county[1] than my brother John and I, but it is more likely there are but few, if any. Our father, C. C. Clayton, moved to the territory composing of this county in November, 1840, and settled the land about five miles east of Tupelo. I was then a very small boy, being some less than four years old, though I remember the move. When we moved to this county the nearest settlement to us on the west was the residence of the Colbert brothers, half-breed Indians,[2] about five miles from Tupelo; and to the east of us the nearest resident was the Hartfield place, about five miles west from Fulton, and no neighbors nearer on the by-roads either north or south of us.

There were no doctors in the country at all, and only occasionally did a Methodist minister pass through on a very wide circuit. My father bled people who wished it done, and extracted their teeth with a pair of pullers which he himself made in his blacksmith shop. No physician entered our home but once the first ten years of our residence here, and the patient whom he attended, a brother younger and next in birth to me, died. When he died no graveyard had been selected in all this country, and we had to bury him in a little lot where we then thought a church would be built, but which was never done, and there his remains rested until the old graveyard was located near the present residence of Eugene Curtis, when we removed his remains to that place. This is the old Bethlehem graveyard, where there was a Cumberland Presbyterian church for many years, and many of my relatives rest under its trees.

When we first settled here the appearance of the country was quite different to what it is now. Game was plentiful, and it was no uncommon thing for deer to walk up to the house or be seen by a short walk into the woods. Wolves, also, and wildcats and catamounts were numerous, and an occasional panther could be heard to scream. I remember one time when I was a small boy to have gone with a woman who lived on our place to visit a neighbor, and, being quite late in the evening returning home, the wolves came howling on our track and near to us as though they would devour us, and the rapidity with which we moved off would have done honor to a quarter horse. There was then in this country a beautiful bird in large droves, but which have since disappeared altogether—they were called paraquites,[3] and were a beautiful green, red and yellow color, with very long crooked bills, somewhat like that of a parrot, and they were very much the size of parrots. There were quite destructive to wheat, oats, and rye fields. There was also a reptile which we called scorpions,[4] and which have also become extinct in this country. They were quite large, as I now remember, some of them eighteen inches long, with a dark and sometimes bright brown color, with a blood red head, and they often made a sound as the barking of a small dog, and I have seen them often jump out of a tree like a squirrel, and we boys used always to believe that they would spring out of trees on us, but such never occurred. There were a great variety of birds then which we never see now, and red birds were then as thick as the English sparrow is now.

The vast forests were covered with the original sage grass, growing as high as a man's head, and interspersed here and there with wild peas and beggar lice, both of which were fine for cattle. In the fall or winter this grass was burned off, and by that means all undergrowth was kept down, so that the woods were set in large forest trees, with open space between, by which any one could see as far as the eye could scan. Some places in the hollows there was switch cane instead of grass above mentioned, and all the bottoms were thickly covered with large cane, among which cattle could winter in good fix. There was a growth of small trees, saplings and bushes on the borders of the streams. In the creeks fish were abundant, and there were many large and deep holes in the creeks, enabling the fish to live all through the dry seasons of the year, which have been filled up in late years by the washing into them of sand and dirt from cultivated fields.

If I had the pen of a ready writer, enabling me to give a pen-picture of the appearance of the virgin forests in these olden times, covered with the great upstretching trees, with occasional vines entwining them from top to bottom, loaded with wild grapes or luscious muscadines, and the plains and hillsides waving with beautiful wild flowers "wasting their fragrance on the desert air," it would read like a fairy tale and be read with the avidity of a school boy's first perusal of *Ivanhoe* or *Rob Roy*.

May 19, 1905

When we first moved to this country, there were no schools of any kind, as the people were so sparsely settled that it was impossible to get enough children together to make a school, and those who had moved in were too poor to have private tutors. I think the first school ever taught in the western part of old Itawamba,[1] where we then lived, was in the year 1844, which school I attended, with three of my older brothers and one sister. This school was taught by a lame man by the name of Lynn. It was what we know now as an "Old Field" school. I remember the appearance of the teacher very well even at this distance of time. He was rather a small man, lame of one leg, walked with crutches, sandy hair, small head, but high forehead, with piercing gray eyes and a countenance anything but attractive. He ruled the school with an iron hand, and almost with an iron rod. I recollect well the kind of rods he had and how he used them. The ferule was the smooth last year's growth of the winter whortleberry, there being no chance near the place to get the hickory, which was much preferable. Many of the pupils had to travel from three to four miles to attend this school, and we among the number. In that school and several others which I attended subsequently, the custom was for every body to "study out" as it was called, each pupil reading or spelling as loud as he might choose, and when the spelling lesson for the evening, commonly called the turn down lesson, was announced, which was done about ten minutes before the pupils took their places in the class for the final spell down of the evening, each child vied with all the others to see who could make most noise, and I have heard such for hundreds of yards; and during this time, the teacher would walk the floor in all his glory, ever and anon deciphering for some little urchin the pronunciation of a word, while he held his book upside down, or slantwise toward the teacher, or, if the teacher was lame and sour, as Lynn was, he sat in his chair with consciousness of his power and importance, and like Alexander Selkirk, realized that he was "monarch of all he surveyed," and often took special pains to let it be known.

Another custom in the olden time, and one that gave many a heart pang to the younger boys, and made the older ones feel their importance, was that of allowing boys over a certain age to go out of the school house under the trees to study their lessons. It was a landmark in a boy's life when, for the first time, he was given permission by the master to take his slate and books and retire beyond the confine of the house for study with the older and larger boys. Sentiments change very much for the better, at least in some respects, as the years go by. I remember one teacher at old Mooreville⁶ who got drunk every Friday after school, and just sobered off ready for business Monday morning and yet he held on to his school for the full term, while now, he would be dismissed for the first offense. This man, whose name I withhold out of delicacy, wrote a beautiful copy, and notwithstanding his debauch from Friday evening till Sunday afternoon when Monday morning came he was ready to furnish you a beautiful copy all the same. We had few books in those olden days. Webster's speller and Smiley's Arithmetic constituted our stock in trade. In those earliest days of our history here, and in the first few schools, we had no readers, and all the reading we did was what we found in the speller, and then we would take up the New Testament, whose English by the way, is transcendent. After attending several schools the word was passed that we must be silent while getting our lessons, and I remember very distinctly that this was considered by all as a great innovation and by many as a great outrage. Books to read in those early times were scarcely thought of by the great mass of the people. I very well know that when I had arrived to the age of fourteen, some few books which I managed to secure in some way published by some tract society in which were the tale of Moses and of Joseph, were read by me with great relish and I trust much profit, too. As for books of poems and works of fiction in those early times, they were never thought of by those early settlers. What would young America now think of such opportunities? And may we not very pertinently ask of him, have you kept pace with your opportunities? I was twenty-one years of age when I saw the first copy of the *Lady of the Lake*, which was then in the hands of Colonel Mitchell, who died here some fifteen years ago, and who was a great lover of Scott's writings.

When I was sixteen years old my life was touched by coming in contact with a Grammar teacher named B. F. Manire, and I shall always look back to the contact and pleasure, and even delight for he directed my attention and thought, young as I then was, to subjects that should engage the best powers of the mind and heart, and fill the hands with work in the constant endeavor to elevate the citizenship of the country. I remember him now as he was then in his youthful appearance, tall, slender, straight as an arrow, rather sallow faced, seemingly almost effeminate, yet lithe and tough, able to stand his hand with the foremost in wrestling and jumping, mild and gentle in his manners, lovable in his disposition and beloved by all his pupils. He was the most accurate grammarian I have ever met, and had a new system which he knew "by heart," as I know the alphabet. He was the first man I ever heard lecture on temperance. I see him now in my mind's eye as he ascends the pulpit to face a full house, largely attracted from curiosity, to hear what a beardless boy could say on such a subject. But the first movement of the man showed the audience that he was master of the situation. Taking in his hand a glass of pure crystal water, he waved it before his hearers, as though it were a heave offering, and said:

> Some like to drink from the foaming brink,
> Where the wine drop's glance they see;
> But water bright in its silver light
> And a crystal cup for me.

Then he gave us a definition of temperance and it clings to me after all these years as if spoken yesterday. "Temperance" said he, "is the moderate use of that which is good, and a total abstinence from that which is evil or bad." He made a fine impression and this was the entering wedge of the temperance movement in our county for the betterment of humanity and for the protection of our youths and for the elevation of our women, which like the little cloud no larger than a man's hand has become a mighty tempest for good, not only in our own county, but has extended far and wide sometimes so rapidly and unexpectedly that some have needed the assistance of another Elijah to get out of the way of it. Ah! how I see the faces of those grammar pupils in that old log house as I sit here and write; seeing them not as they now are, but as they then appeared, beautiful and lovely young ladies, strong and chivalrous young men, I only being so young as sixteen full of life and hope, just entering on life's real journey, having no conception and but little thought for what was in store for them. I will not name them now, but should I do so, the friends would be saying all along the line as the names should be read, "she was called over the river many years ago"; "the footfalls of the dread messenger came to him amid the quiet walks of life before the war began"; "yes, I remember well the spot where the swift messenger of death in the enemy's bullet came to him on the bloody field of Shiloh." Some few linger, like the last trees of the field, waiting for the call home. When I think of these old friends and comrades of the old grammar school, it touches a tender chord in my heart, and draws me toward the old spot just south of old Mooreville, and though I knew it has been so long that all who survive are aged now, yet, when they appear to my vision they are still clad in the habiliment of youth and beauty.

May 26, 1905

How long the Indians roamed over these magnificent forests, and looked upon these great uplifting and overtopping poplar, walnut, chestnut, hickory, oak and gum trees, and chased the deer and shot the wild turkey with his bow and arrow, speared the fish in the wild-wooded streams and cultivated his little patch of maize by the side of the wigwam, no man will ever know. They wrote no history, however much they may have made. But when they left this country in 1836, they left to the white man the same virgin forest they had enjoyed so long, save the little maize clumps beside their lodges, the deer roaming over the hills and valleys as of yore, the trout in the lake, the birds amid the trees, and the furrow unturned. What a lovely picture to look upon had we in those olden days! What a view for a landscape painter to set his cultivated eye upon! About the time we came here and soon thereafter, great herds of cattle could have been seen grazing upon the wide stretch of native grassplains and small prairies, with a deer occasionally slipping away from them, and which could be seen sometimes for almost or quite a mile, the country being open, and nothing to obstruct the view, save the great trunks of the forest trees. But year by year and month by month the pioneer pushed in, and began filling in the space, and the forest fires became less and less frequent and the present growth that now so thickly covers the woodlands began springing up and filling in the vacant places, and the axe of the settler felled the great trees, making them into boards and rails, and occasionally into plank by means of the whip saw.

Many of my readers doubtless have never seen a whip saw at work, and so I will describe it. The whip saw is a straight saw having a handle at each end, not like the common cross-cut saw, but entering through the saw laterally and extending an equal distance on each side of the blade. In order to saw, the log is elevated upon a scaffolding so high that a man can stand straight under it; then two men do the sawing, one on top the log and the other underneath, the man on the ground having his face covered with a veil to protect his eyes from the saw dust. By this means did our fathers procure what plank they then used. I have often seen my father and my oldest brother thus sawing lumber and longed for the time when I should be large enough to handle the saw myself, but I never did. It passed out of use before I arrived to manhood. In the early days we always broke out lands for corn with the bulltongue plow and crossed it off and dropped the corn the same way we first ran with the plow in running it off, and covered with the hoe. The cotton was drilled,[7] but covered with two furrows with the bulltongue and knocked off with a board or home-made wooden harrow. The corn was worked till silking and tasseling. One of the good old customs, I have often thought, might have been kept up, but which disappeared many years ago, was "corn shucking." It was then customary for each neighbor to make a "corn shucking," invite his friends, and they would come in crowds, and shuck out all his corn, the good women at the same time having a quilting, and by these means the men and women of the neighborhood would often get together and spend many pleasant hours. The husking often extended into the night and was generally crowned by placing a darkey on the corn pile to lead the song while the other negroes present would join in the chorus. Their happy, joyous countenances, their weird expressions and their deep bass voices, mingled with an occasional scream from the screech owl, was a thing not to be forgotten and especially when the negro minstrel, at the hooting of the owl, would often stop his leadership, and break out, "Nigger, you hear dat bird? Time we gittin' 'way from dis place. Shore gwine ter be

somethin' done. Le' me down from here." So, with the corn shucking and the quilting gatherings and the log rollings and the young
peoples' parties, there was much social intercourse between the
different neighborhoods, and life passed in a pleasant and joyous
manner. As the years rolled on and the country became more
thickly settled, church facilities increased and were fairly good, the
preacher, however, ordinarily working in the field, or giving his
attention to merchandise during the week, and dispensing the Word
from the sacred desk on the Sabbath; but there were no Sabbath
schools. I was a grown young man before I ever had an opportunity
of attending a Sabbath school.

Up to some time in the fifties, there were but few renters in the
country. Almost all owned their farms and if anyone did not own a
home, he ordinarily worked for wages or "overseered" for someone
having slaves.

Very few white women then worked in the fields. They kept the
house, spun the thread, wove the cloth and made clothes for the
family and bed clothing for the beds, including as beautiful counter-
pieces as my eyes ever beheld. They also dyed wool with walnut
bark and made lovely homespun winter wear for the men and boys
and with different colors made a kind of woolen linsey for their
own underwear.

The farmer raised everything he needed for home consumption,
except sugar, coffee and molasses, and a supply of that was laid in
once a year when the crop was sold. Wheat was raised in abundance
for home use and I never saw a barrel of flower[8] till in the fifties.
But no sorghum was raised till about 1854, but some molasses were
made in parts of the country from maple water, however only in a
few places.

Fire hunting was common. May be you don't know what that is
and how conducted. Well, the vessel carrying the fire and light was
made by crossing iron strips, bending and fastening them to another
strip at the top, thus making an oblong open pan, say twelve by
eighteen inches and about a foot deep. This pan was attached to a
long handle by which to carry it. The light was made by burning
rich pine in the pan, which was carried on the shoulder of the fire

hunter, the pan in his rear and having someone along as an assistant to carry the gun and the supply of lightwood for the trip and look after the dog, if one was carried. The game thus hunted was deer, and they were discovered by the shining of their eyes, which look like two great stars. The deer seem to be entranced by the light and will permit the hunter to get so close to him that his body may be readily seen. The usual course is for the assistant to carry the gun and extra wood for the fire, walking at the heels of the hunter until he sights the deer's eyes; and he then simply reaches back his hand for the gun saying nothing, and the assistant hands him the gun, takes hold of the dog and never moves again until the gun fires. Deer were in the habit of assembling to lick salty places of earth, where such salty earth could be found, which was generally on white, sandy soil at the head of hollows or ravines, and there the fire hunter generally found them. I remember to have gone with my brother, John, on Saturday night and again on Monday following, and we never went over half a mile from the house, and yet we carried in a fine doe Saturday night and a nice buck on Monday night. The shot just creased the buck, and but for the faithful old dog, we would have lost him, but the dog held the deer down till another shot was fired into his head. This fire hunting was pretty dangerous to horses and cows, as it took a practiced hand to distinguish the eye of a horse or cow from that of a deer, and many an unlucky wight has been very much crestfallen over his mistake and that to his neighbor's sorrow. But fire hunting, like the deer of the forest, is a thing of the past.

June 2, 1905

I desire to say to you readers, that unless I thought these "Pen Pictures" were read by many with interest, I surely would not go to the trouble and labor to prepare them. Writing is not now as easily done with me as it could have been done forty years ago in the vigor of my young manhood, when my brow was free from crows feet, and my hair untouched by the silver thread; as no wavery word penned is written with both hands holding the pen that traces the lines. I wish also to say that these pictures are not painted for all whose eyes may rest upon them. Some men are so busy with buying and selling, adding and counting interest, and thinking of profit and loss, and some so absorbed in their farms and their crops, and even on dull days and rainy seasons, they have not time to read anything like the items I write. There is no money in it to them, and by money they measure everything. I write for two classes of readers, those who have leisure to devote to reading, and like to do so; and those busy ones who, notwithstanding the emergency of labor and business employments, will take time to read some any way.

A little incident occurred while I was attending school at old Richmond[9] in 1856 which convinced me that people will enjoy word picturing if done in a natural way and in plain English free from Latin, French, or other foreign language, which they do not understand. We had a public examination and Composition reading at the close of the spring session and I wrote a composition on an imaginary country, called "Buncom," describing its hills and val-leys, mountains and rocks, rooks and rills, its fields of waving grain, the flowers of its spring and the beauty of its scenery in the hazy months of October and November, all tinted with purple and gold and carnation with the farm houses dotting the hill sides and climbing up the foot hills of the mountains, and the smoke rising from the dwellings, the lowing cattle browsing on the meadows, and the fowls cackling round the barnyard. I read it to brother James, who was attending the same school. "Well," said he, "I'll people that country for you in my Composition." And so he wrote a composition in which he described the inhabitants of "Buncom," their dwellings, their dress and manners, the kind of occupations they followed, how they cultivated their fields, their social gather-ings, and the kind of food they ate. We indicated to the teacher that our compositions were connected and which one should be read first. We captivated the house and yet there were many composi-tions read that day which, for thought and expression, were equal, and probably superior to them, but it was that simple narrative style which pleased. Now, if after all these years, I can confine my word painting to the same simple style, and remain true to nature, I shall not lack for readers.

The first political campaign I remember was that for president in 1844. The contest was between the Whigs and Democrats, James K. Polk and George M. Dallas being the Democratic leaders and Henry Clay and Freeling Huysen[10] the Whig leaders. The contest was very exciting, and often the respective followers came to blows. I remember very well that all the Democrats who passed our house with wagons, and the wagon was then the chief means of transportation, had their harness painted with poke berries.

As the people moved in and settled up the country, and the forests were felled, the corn and wheat and cotton planted, the stores opened and the blacksmith shop established, the doctors and lawyers settled in their practice, there also came along with them the liquor traffic. In all the towns of any size there was from one to three "groceries," as they were then called, where liquor was sold by the drink, and in addition to this, at every place where anything else was sold, the beverage could be bought by the gallon, and at many cross roads nothing was sold but liquor. The whiskey could be bought for forty cents a gallon, and I suppose as good quality as you can now buy for two dollars and a half. A dime each would furnish four men a gallon, and then such drinking as they had, for you must know they did not buy it to divide and carry home for medicine,[11] but to drink somewhere on the ground. In my raising it was a general thing for the men to visit saloons and drink whiskey. Few men would refuse a drink. Do you ask, "how was drunkenness then compared with now?" You would then see a dozen drunk men where you will not see one now. At old Mooreville and Richmond, on Saturdays and public days, you would frequently see men lying on the corners down, and many more still going but staggering and swearing as they went. It was very seldom men refused a drink when offered, but I must say my father always refused to drink "with the boys," and I never saw him take a drink nor did I ever hear of his doing so.

One of the old time institutions I must not forget, and that is the stage coach. It was one of the last of the olden time institutions to give way before advancing improvements. When the stage coach arrived in the towns and hamlets, it was like the coming in of a railroad train now, so far as the excitement of the curious is concerned. The driver who was at once conductor and engineer, brakeman and fireman, often felt his power and importance. As he came into the towns and villages where he was to change his team, he sounded his bugle blast clear and keen, dashed in at better speed, and cracked his whip, turned his team over to the hostler whose business it was to take and replace them with fresh horses, and himself strode away for a drink and his meal. The old stage coach was never supposed to be full, but to hold one more, either inside or on top, and the movements of the great old thing were like that of a ship at sea, and many had "stage sickness" from riding in or on it. It was one of the last relics of the olden time, only giving way to this country just before the civil war. But, until the railroads came, it was the only means of public travel unless the trip could be made by water. In those olden times all our cotton was flat boated on the river to Mobile, New Orleans or Memphis, after being hauled to the river side. It was very inconvenient, and often the river did not rise till in the spring and sometimes not at all. I have known my father to sell cotton in New Orleans after waiting months for returns at four cents per pound.

June 16, 1905

Before I write what I have to say in this article, I wish to state that a wee tiny bird, less than any bird except the humming bird, has come to our home since I began writing these Pen Pictures, hopping from limb to limb, and flitting from tree to tree, trilling her beautiful music, as if to say, "I give you this for the songs of the birds of long ago which you have lost and mourned for in these articles. Receive me for the new and mourn no more for the old."

In those early times it was somewhat difficult to start a fire if we should let the "seed" go out. The rekindling was done by means of a piece of cotton, or more usually dry punk,[12] placed on a flint, and striking it with the back of a pocket knife until the sparks should set the cotton or punk on fire, and then carefully applying some easily combustible substance till a fire should be kindled. Sometimes it would take almost or quite half an hour thus to start up a fire.

Lights were quite primitive. Sometimes lights for the kitchen, and even the dining table, were made by dipping a piece of cloth cut into a string into an earthen vessel with a kind of small lip to it, where the end of the thread-made wick rested, the vessel being filled with lard, or some kind of oil and setting the lip end on fire. It made a dim, poor light, but better than none. Then we had the home-made tallow candles, which were made four to six at a time by pouring melted tallow into tin molds, into which had been placed threads for wicks, connected together at the top by a small rod of wood, the points of the wicks having been carefully drawn through the small holes at the ends tapered to a point in the shape of the ordinary candle you now see. After the molds had stood till the candles were thoroughly hard, by a little warming up, they could be readily lifted out, looking slick and greasy. This candle made a very fair light, and such as I have read by often. But in the winter time the primitive light was the pine knots lying on the pine hills seemed to be common property, and he who wished went and hauled for family use.

In the early forties wheat was cut with a reap hook, being a crooked blade instrument, with rough edge, sharpened with a rough or coarse rock, and the handle of the hook was about ten inches long, and the cutting was done with one hand, while the swath of wheat to be cut was held with the other hand. And as little as you may think of it, an expert with the hook claimed that he would not be much behind the man with the scythe.

Houses were generally built of logs and hewn down with the broad axe after being raised. Sometimes the logs were lined and hewn on the ground, if the party wished to make an extra nice log house. Poplar is the best tree with which to make this kind of house, and in the early forties they were plentiful. The floors were made of puncheons, being logs split the whole width of the tree, and then dressed off with the adze.[13] The covering was generally four-feet boards, either oak or cypress. The cabins for the negroes were generally in the rear of the main dwelling, of one room each, and set in rows. It wasn't safe for a darkey to be found out from home without a pass, and if so found, the patrols, those self-appointed regulators for the neighborhood, would be very apt to give him a regulation whipping.

Kindness toward the slaves in the olden time was the rule, but occasional cases of cruelty could be found. Slaves would "run away," as it was called, once in awhile, and have to be hunted by dogs. I remember one instance in the forties when some "run away" came to our kitchen and smokehouse one night, and cooked and carried off enough to do him several weeks. Some negroes were fierce and determined, and would fight the dogs until overpowered, and then generally received a thrashing for their resistance. Colonel Dabbs, who lived some miles southeast of old Richmond had a pack of "nigger hounds" that were extra fine and he claimed that if he could get to the starting place of the run away in twenty four hours after he had left he was sure of his man. Many, and even most of the negroes, had many enjoyments with each other. A 'possum or a coon hunt was an occasion of much pleasure to them. And then when a big, fine, fat 'possum had been killed and properly dressed, flanked with nice sweet potatoes, swimming in his own grease, and came before the darkey for proper consideration and dispatch, that was the highest conception of life of which he was capable. The gatherings which they occasionally had, when the old-time fiddle was brought into requisition, and they engaged in the dance, was to them the sweetest and best of living. And such dancing as some of those old-time darkies could do was worth looking at. The many twists and turns, and the back step, and the graceful, circling movement, with the bending of the body forward and then backward, and then darting across the room, ever pursued one by another and still ever the one eluding the others. The dreamy croon of the old, old mammy darkey, in which she hummed partly to herself and partly to those around, and in which she made her song as she went, with its weird sweetness, was only permitted to one generation, and has now passed away forever. This old, old mammy negro, having served her master and mistress faithfully and long, and being now too old to work, and not being able to read, nor any of her race capable of reading to her, thus sat in her corner whiling away her time with little patch-work and dreaming of the coming time, and meanwhile singing these simple, far-away sounding bits of song. Then there was old black mammy, not so old, but old enough to be freed from hard work of the field, and who was entrusted with the care of the mistress' children, and thought infinitely more of the white children than of her own, and to whom the children of the household looked up as almost a savior, for she was ready at all times to take their part, and shield them from every harm and protect them from all danger.

When the war came up and young master, whom black mammy had brought up, was called to the front, she wanted some "nasty, triflin' nigger" to go along and wait on him, and see that no harm came to him.

As a general thing the master and mistress and their slaves lived in congenial association, the whites being kind and gentle to the slaves, and they loving and willingly serving their owners. And so when the wonderful civil war came to desolate our homes, the slaves as a general thing remained at home while the masters went to war, and worked the farms and cared for the women and children, and mourned over the master when killed as if he were more even than a father to them.

In those olden times the darkey was well provided for, so that no thought of how he should live and what on ever passed through his mind, and his clothing was furnished him, and the doctor and medicine at hand without his knowing anything about it, and there being therefore no cares on his mind we find but very few insane ones before their freedom. I do not remember of a single instance of a demented slave. The joyous song and the hilarious laugh was common among the slaves, and nit a carking care came to "roll across their peaceful breast," except what may have disturbed them thinking and hoping for freedom. Liberty being the natural state of all mankind, I suppose the negro slaves longed for freedom, as the red man of the forest wistfully looked for a return of the unbounded range of the forest when confined in a narrow compass.

October 20, 1905

In 1854, as best my memory serves me, Ben Johnson taught a school at old Andrews Chapel, then in Itawamba county. About the time he left the Andrews Chapel neighborhood, he was taken with a very severe cough, and both he and his friends thought he had tuberculosis. This lasted for several years, and he then began to mend of that; but soon thereafter he had a wonderful trouble with his liver, and his tongue was coated like a man with typho-malarial fever, except that the coating on the tongue was very white. He also suffered very much. This lasted during the entire war and for several years afterwards, when he began suffering intense pain in the side of his back, and he was prostrated on his bed for a long while. Finally, the hurting in his back developed into a boil as the doctors thought and declared. Some days after the boil was lanced there came floating out through the boil an ordinary sized sewing needle; and this needle had been the cause of all his suffering for all these years, being about thirteen years in all. I saw him only a short time after the needle floated out, and saw the needle with the short cut thread still in it, and remember very well how it looked so soon as the needle came out, Johnson got well, and had not more trouble.

August 11, 1905

I remember well a beautiful little valley just east of Richmond where the boys and girls used to congregate on Saturdays and gather "sweet Williams" and violets in the Springtime and in the time of the sear and fallen leaf weave together the green, the yellow, the red, the purple, and the carnation from the forest and make chaplets a prince might be proud to wear. The great overhanging trees of the valley, without undergrowth, and the wide expanse of the scenery north and south of the public highways was a lovely one to behold. It reminded me very much of the valley south and near our old home, which before the axe and hoe penetrated its quiet precincts, filled with its sugar maple, poplar, magnificent oaks, and beautiful red bud and white blooming dogwood, was really a gem of beauty. But now, as I pass them both by I find that cotton and corn grow in all the places where nature's handiwork so beautified the landscape in the long ago. I remember well when I was a small boy trying to be at the hickory tree before the hogs got there to gather the falling fruit on the hills north of the old home, but they were always there before me crunching the nuts, however early I might be there. That beautiful rolling landscape is now a thick mat of undergrowth, with all of its pastime beauty and loveliness gone.

NOTES

[1] Lee County, Mississippi, formerly Itawamba County.

[2] Descendants of the prominent Chickasaw family of the area, most of whom moved west to new territories in 1837-8.

[3] The Carolina Paroquet, now extinct.

[4] The red-headed "scorpion" is the second largest of the Broad-Headed Skink group of reptiles.

[5] Itawamba County, Mississippi, part of which became Lee County.

[6] Eight miles east of Tupelo, also referred to by Clayton as Mooresville.

[7] Sown by being dropped along a shallow furrow.

[8] Flour.

[9] A small settlement, 1830-60, 5 miles south of Mooreville.

[10] Theodore Frelinghuysen.

[11] Drug stores also sold whiskey, but were not supposed to sell it unless it was prescribed by a physician as medicine.

[12] Dry decayed wood.

[13] Cutting tool with thin blade set at right angles to the handle, used to shape wood.

CHAPTER II

A Young Man Sets Out
1855–1859

> . . . there's nothing so hard as the beginning,
> unless, perhaps, the end.

THE PERSONAL HISTORY that Clayton relates in the articles of this chapter is typical of any time and any place—the initiation into the world of a young man setting out to make a living. Sometimes the going is rough. Young Clayton obviously must quit school because of finances, having "pressed the credit system about as far as a man should expect any one to look upon him with favor in that direction." As the older Clayton looks back on his early attempts to gain a teaching position, he finds amusement in his youthful naiveté. He pictures himself as a young bumpkin ill prepared for his first employment interview; and in describing his flagging confidence following his first job refusal, he links himself with young persons everywhere.

Yet, like most young men, Clayton does eventually make his way in the world—from the male academy at Old Richmond, to a school of his own in northern Alabama, then back to Mississippi to become a self-taught, circuit-riding young lawyer. As he recounts the tribulations of his early years, it is the older Clayton's ability to laugh at the younger version of himself which gives these articles a double dimension and renders them timelessly enjoyable.

Also woven into this narrative are Clayton's laments over the demise of Old Richmond, the "Deserted Village" of northeast Mississippi, and site of his happy days at Martin's Male Academy. As he elegizes the extinct community in elevated, archaic language, we again sense Clayton's attachment to the past and deep sense of loss at its irretrievability.

The articles in this chapter thus reflect the mixed tone of levity and seriousness found in many of these "Pen Pictures of the Olden Time." There is certainly much to amuse us in this chapter, but Clayton's is a gentle humor which easily shifts to nostalgia. In these articles, Clayton smiles at his own boyish inexperience, but the passage of that youthful time and the demise of the trustworthy markers of a smaller, more stable world he cannot help but lament.

July 14 & 23, 1905

In September, 1855, I began attending school, at old Richmond then in Itawamba but now in Lee county. Richmond, how can I write of thee, after the lapse of these fifty years! When I put my pen to the paper to write of thee, the crowding scenes of thy busy life and thy happy days; thy beautiful and lovely women and thy brave and chivalrous men; thy black headed male teacher, kind and gentle, loving and true, noble and generous, an honor to his profession and a friend to humanity; and thy graceful and queenly teaching of the young ladies of that olden time; thy hills and vales and intertwining chaparral between; thy noble merchants and learned physicians; thy rows of business houses, with their crowded contents; thy bright and joyous children, overflowing the schools, and thy churches filled with happy worshippers from Sabbath to Sabbath, and the old time darkey-slave, sleek and prim, in charge of the family carriage, but sitting in the corner of the old church—these, all these, and much more rise up before me with their crowning beauty and interest like an oasis in the desert to the wayworn, thirsty traveler, or like the "shadow of a great rock in a weary land," to the foot-sore and wayworn soldier! But, dear old Richmond, when I now revisit thy former beauty and loveliness, these visions disappear like the will o'wisp, leaving nothing but corn and cotton fields instead of the vision, and with the poet we may truly say:

> Sweet, smiling village, loveliest of the lawn,
> Thy sports are fled, and all thy charms withdrawn.[1]

And taking out the "hawthorn" from the poet's sad and mournful song of wailing, and substituting in its place "redhaw," and we may again repeat:

> Where once the cottage stood, the redhaw grew,
> Remembrance wakes with all her busy train,
> Swells at my breast, and turns the past to pain.
> To thee no more the peasant shall repair,
> To sweet oblivion of his daily care.

And at the old Inn, where the rule was that joy should be unconfined,

> The host himself no longer shall be found
> Careful to see the mantling bliss go round;
> Nor the coy maid, half willing to be prest,
> Shall kiss the cup to pass it to the rest.

And methinks, as the new was coming into view, and preparing to push out and destroy the old, some old timer, who had seen thee in sunshine and in shade, and who was anxious that thou mightst live on through the ages to come, and who "In conscious virtue brave, / He only wished for worlds beyond the grave," bade thee farewell with many a tender tear, and never saw the beauty, and the glory of the incoming new, but always longed for the halcyon days of the old, until the quiet footfalls of the messenger showed him the real grandeur and joy of the new up yonder.

June 23, 1905

I write also wholly from memory, having kept no diary of transactions in these olden times. Richmond was a gay place then, and attracted more visitors and was a better town even than the capital of the county.[2] The people in the surrounding country were well-to-do farmers, owning many slaves and plantations, and many of them often came to town and put up at the old hotel and spent considerable time with their friends there while their overseers attended to their farming interests. It was a very social place. The men generally had leisure and the women no cares. The lawyers attended the Justice Courts there from Fulton, as if it had been a Circuit Court, and well they might, for there was much business requiring their services. Rhoden W. Palmer was the justice of the peace then, and for years before and for many years after, and Colonel W. M. Pound, who married my sister, was the constable. In the month of December 1855, I assisted Colonel Pound in riding for the January term of the Justice Court, and there were something over three hundred cases heard at that term. The business of collecting was worth money to the lawyers in those days. For instance a lawyer was entrusted with a lot of claims for collection, and he would see the debtor, and he in turn would deliver to the lawyer collaterals to cover his own debt, and the lawyer would collect the collaterals, apply the proceeds to the discharge of the original claim, and thus receive pay from his client for collecting his debt, and from the debtor for collecting his collaterals. Nor was a debtor broke every time a lot of claims were placed in the hands of a lawyer against him, neither were the exemption laws so covering then as to shield a debtor from paying his debts. Such a thing as making an assignment for the benefit of his creditors was never heard of in those days, but when a man got into financial trouble he used every means as a general thing to pay out and take a new start. I remember a little incident that occurred with me and a debtor on whom Colonel Pound had a claim for collection that was really amusing. He was a man of means, but like some men whom you find now, always seemed to think the next call will do as well. I was only eighteen, a beardless boy, and Colonel Pound told me this man would not be likely to pay, but that he would make the excuse that he had no small bills, the claim being about twenty dollars. So he supplied me with plenty of change so I could accommodate his excuse. When I approached him for payment he said, "All my bills are big ones." I asked the size of the smallest bill, and he very readily said that the least bill he had was one hundred dollars, supposing of course that I would not be able to do anything with it. But, thanks to Colonel Pound's providence, I was enabled to say very promptly, "I am prepared to break that," and so there was no further excuse. I have thought it more than likely that if he had been posted about the contents of my pocketbook he would have had nothing under a five hundred dollar bill!

I must not fail to give some further account of that grand old man, Rhoden W. Palmer, Esq. In the first place, he was one of the best, if not the very best, justices of the peace I have known. He had a fine judicial mind and would have made a fine lawyer and a most excellent judge if he had been educated to the bar. He knew no man when it came to investigating cases, but held the scales of justice with blinded eyes, and rendered his judgement as the testimony required and his sense of justice dictated. He was much in favor of calling in equity to aid him in his decisions, especially where he was somewhat in doubt as to the law, holding to the theory that if abstract justice was done between man and man, the law ought not to be far missed. His kindness toward the bar and all litigants was proverbial. I used to go to his house in the winter of 1855–56 by direction of Colonel Pound to get process to be served, and have seen him many a time sitting out under a shed in the yard, the smoke curling around his head from the open fire, with the old gold pen that he had used for almost or quite a quarter of a century, writing summonses in a most beautiful handwriting, and thus he sat for days together, writing out everything in full, having no blanks, and when his docket was made up it would compare favorably with any clerk's docket in the state.

July 28, 1905

Some merchants only last for a season, and many only for a little longer time. But in old Richmond in 1855 there was a firm of merchants doing business then under the names of Raymond and Trice, composed of Alfred H. Raymond and Robert L. Trice. I dealt with Raymond and Trice from 1855, more or less, for many years and I must say I never dealt with more square and accommodating gentlemen than they; and then when you owed them and could not pay, all they asked of you was good faith and an honest effort to pay, and they would indulge you as long as you could ask. They collected their debts without suit, and you always thought, in dealing with them, you were in the house of your friends. When I went to Richmond, I was not quite nineteen, a poor boy without means, and even having no money with which to pay board, clothing and books, and I must say the merchants and those with whom I boarded treated me superbly, and Raymond and Trice were among them, for they all sold me on credit, and Colonel W. M. Pound and J. B. White with whom I boarded, never asked me for a dollar; and in the fall of 1856, after eating their grub and wearing clothes for fifteen months, I went on an unexpected visit with my uncle to Jefferson county, Alabama, and finding a good school awaiting me there, I came not again till in the fall of 1857, and yet not one of them all ever wrote me they wished their money. Those were the good old times of long ago. Who would not joyfully pay such men, and remember them too with gratitude all these years? Who can beat the record?

Old Richmond scored it with me. I never pass her deserted site, but I remember the kindness of hers to me in the long ago.

August 25, 1905

In the fall of 1856, having no money, and thinking I had pressed the credit system about as far as a man should expect any one to look upon him with favor in that direction, I started out from old Richmond, armed with a well written recommendation from my old teacher, Henry Martin, to seek a school.³ It was the first time I had ever gone out to seek business for myself, and I was quite awkward in that role. The first place I stopped was at Colonel Joe Hill's who then lived at the place now owned and occupied by Joe Clark, in Shannon, but it was a farm house then, and there was no town of Shannon then in existence. Colonel Hill was a sedate, stately old gentleman of the old school "befo' the wa'" kind, and rather particular as to the qualifications of the man who should teach his children, and being a kind of leader in the neighborhood, felt that he was even responsible as to who should teach their school whether he had pupils to send or not. I think Colonel Hill was like a great many people are even now, looking largely to the kind of clothes a man wears to find out what kind of a man the wearer is. I was a boy then, less than twenty, and had on only common clothing, suitable to a poor man, though they were clean and respectable, but I remember I wore a fuzzy quilled cap, and it was rather large for my head and came down rather low on my ears, and I guess, on the whole, I was rather a tough looking customer to be applying for a school. Colonel Hill was a very dignified looking old gentleman, and while very polite, and what the world would call kind, yet his politeness and kindness was of that kind which, while you could have no objection to it, seemed to hold you at a distance. When I made known my business, Colonel Hill was not long in informing me that they wanted a man who could teach a "High School," and I drew the conclusion right readily, though he did not say so, that I was not the man that he, and consequently the people, wanted to teach their High School. My recommendation from Martin would not work with him with my cap over my ears, and my boyish face. Ever since those days I have had great sympathy for the boys just starting in any kind of business or profession in which they have to look to the public for success, and where I find a worthy young man offering for office, I am his friend, and I think the young lawyers will say I have been especially kind to them through all the years of my professional life, and ready at all times to lend them a helping hand. I left Colonel Hill with a pretty strong impression on my mind that there was not only no school for me in his neighborhood, but I was almost of the opinion that I was neither fit nor competent to teach. I put in the balance of the day looking and listening for some other place in which the people wanted a young man just out of school to "teach the young idea how to shoot," but I found none. That night I put up with Old Ben Rook, who then lived at the first house north of Town Creek on what was then the Ellistown road, and since known as the Poor House place. Both he and his wife were born aristocrats, and he had spent a fortune, but he was especially kind to me and his wife was a very motherly old woman. I showed Uncle Ben my recommendation from Captain

Martin and he scanned it very carefully, and I remember well, through all these years, the objection he made to it. Martin said in the paper that I had assisted him in his school and had given entire satisfaction, and that this was an "earnest" of what I would do with a school of my own. Uncle Ben did not think the word "earnest" was the one which ought to have been used to express the idea intended to be conveyed by the writer. However, after I explained to him that the writer was a fine Latin, Greek and French scholar, in addition to his acquirements in English, he thought it probably the right word. But after my experience with Mr. Rook's doubting of the wording of my recommendation and Colonel Hill's wish for a man of more learning, I thought it best to go back to the land of my birth to make a beginning in life, knowing that "there's nothing so hard as the beginning, unless, perhaps, the end."

After I had gone elsewhere and taught school one year, it was no longer any trouble to teach in the Rook neighborhood, which I did in connection with my brother, J. S. Clayton. At the time I went into that neighborhood, there then lived there some very worthy old timers. As brother James had a family and I had not, it fell to my lot to go home with the children to see the parents in their homes, and remain over night with them and eat out of their baskets with them the next day at noon. In this way I saw much of the home life of the people.

August 18 & October 20, 1905

And now dear old Richmond, I must bid thee farewell, but before I do so wilt thou answer me these questions? Where now are the fair maidens and noble young men who flashed across thy threshold like meteors in the long ago? Where are the heads of families who inhabited thy precincts and the country immediately surrounding thee in 1855 and 1856? How many still remain? In thy desolation and ruin thou canst not answer. Then I must say that of all of those whom I knew in 1855 and 1856 who were heads of families, none remain. Richmond, the pleasant and happy days I have spent among thy haunts and with thy noble young men and lovely maidens, thy matrons and men of old age, shall linger with me as a benediction while my head shall be above the wave. I now bid thee a long adieu, and must look to other scenes and other men and women. In the fall of 1856 I thought I had trespassed upon the good nature and kindness of my friends as long as I ought to, or as in conscience I could. So I left school at Richmond, and my uncle from Alabama being on a visit to my father, I returned with him to his home in Jefferson county, not with the expectation, at that time, however, of remaining long. But after getting to my uncle's home, he thought he could work me up a school out there, and did assist me in making up a fine subscription school, and which I taught for nine months, making money enough to support me that year and to pay up all my expenses at old Richmond for the time I went to school there. While I was making up the school I taught in Alabama in 1857, I approached a middle aged man who was himself a school teacher, and asked him to subscribe to my school. He looked me in the face, and remarked in a rather cutting way, "You are too young to teach school." Uncle had posted me about him before I went to him, so that I felt my way pretty secure, and I simply replied, "My friend, I have seen some old men who couldn't teach school." He did not subscribe but sent all the while and changed his opinion, and was as good friend as I had.

When I had made up my school in Alabama and stood my examination, I had one month at my disposal before my school began, which was January 1, 1857, thus giving me the month of December, 1856 for work or play. I had no money, and so decided to work, if any body would give me any employment. I found a cousin who had a new ground to clear, and prepare it for cultivation, and I worked the month of December in that new ground with him for eleven dollars, which was all the money I had in 1857 until I collected up my school money in September. A little incident occurred while Uncle and I were on our way to his home in 1856 which I will mention. The trip was made on horseback, and on the third day as we were riding along, a gentleman overtook us who lived in the neighborhood where we were then traveling, and introduced himself to us and rode with us some hours. He was a great talker and Uncle and I generally kept silent and let him do the talking. He

spoke of his acquirements in Literature and learning, and especially
spoke of the difficulty of becoming a critical grammarian, but indicated to us very distinctly that he had accomplished that feat, to his
satisfaction at least, but remarked in passing, that the most difficult
thing he encountered in English Grammar was to learn how to
properly use the little words, "these" and "those." "But," says he,
"I have no trouble with them now at all, and can tell you so you will
never be troubled with them. I can illustrate it to you," he went on,
"so you can understand it better in that way than if I were to give
you the rules by which to be governed in the use of these words.
For instance, if there were a number of men out yonder at a distance, and I wished to speak of them, if there were three or more of
them I would say *those* men, but if only two I would say *these*
men!"

My uncle was no grammarian, having never studied it, but his
good judgement and common sense told him how much the gentleman had missed the mark, and it was so ridiculous that we could not
keep back the big ha! ha! The gentleman gave me a very hearty and
cordial invitation to spend the night with him at his father's house as
I returned.

Taking advantage of his invitation, as I returned in the fall of
1857, I spent the night with him. Next morning we went out to the
lot, looking after the horses, and he began telling me of the wonderful peculiarities of an old gray horse belonging to his father, which
was walking around in the lot without having his breakfast, he
having been deprived of his feeding place in order to accommodate
my horse. The gentleman said to me: "This old horse is a great
bluff. He will make out he is going to tear you to pieces, but there is
no danger in him whatever. If you motion at him with your head or
make mouths at him like a colt does, he will run at you as though he
would bite you all to pieces, but he always takes care to stop just
before he gets to you. I will show you how he acts," said he, and
with that, he stuck out his mouth towards the old gray horse,
making mouths like a colt. For some reason probably because he
had been deprived of his stable and his morning's meal, he seemed
to be in a very ill humor, and with all the power and viciousness of

his horseship, he ran at the young man, knocking him down and scooping off a streak of flesh from his shoulder about as wide as two fingers. Although it looked a little squally at the time, it was really a laughable incident to see the old gaunt gray horse standing there with his ears laid back, and the young man acting the colt, and then the dash of the horse, and, when the gentleman saw too late that the horse meant business this time, and his frantic efforts to get to safety, made a picture that any painter would have been glad to have beheld.

In the fall of 1857, brother James and I made an arrangement by which we were to teach together a school south of where Colonel S. H. Taylor then lived for the year 1858, and we called the place Martin Academy in honor of our Richmond teacher, Henry Martin. Among the boarders was a young man not far from my age by the name of Kellis Moorman, now an eminent physician in Alabama. He and I got into a little trouble and misunderstanding at the school house one day, and I treated him pretty harshly, and made him leave the school. On reflecting over the matter, I saw I had acted hastily and treated him harshly and unjustly. I went to his boarding house, some two miles away, and said to him in the reputed language of George Washington, "Kellis, it is natural to err, but it is glory to rectify. I was wrong yesterday, I wish to be right today. I am very sorry indeed that I mistreated you yesterday at the school house. I beg your pardon and ask your forgiveness. If you grant it, and see proper to return to the school, I will treat you as if this had never occurred." He accepted my apology, returned to the school, and was ever after as fast friend as I ever had. In 1858 in that old neighborhood all the patrons of the school owned the land where they lived, and I do not think there was a renter in the neighborhood. It was really an ideal settlement. In the fall of 1858, I left the school and moved to Fulton to study law, while brother James continued the school another year or two longer.

November 3, 1905

About the first of January, 1859 I moved to Fulton in Itawamba county to take up the study of law, having read a little in Blackstone before then. James L. Finley also began the study of law at the same time and place, he occupying the offices of Owen and Owen, and I that of Bullard and Mitchener. Finley was one year older than I, and I was then twenty two, and I am very sure no two country men ever went to the study of the law knowing less in respect to what would be required of us. In those olden times it was not considered necessary that the applicant for admittance to the bar should be even well grounded in legal principles, much less be considered learned in the law. The usual course for admission to the practice was to remain in a lawyer's office for a time and study law, and do such writing for the firm with whom the applicant was studying as might be desired. If the young man was of good moral character, and showed some aptness for the law, he had no difficulty in securing a license to practice. I doubt if Owen and Owen paid out but little attention to the progress Finley was making, and I know Bullard and Mitchener gave no special attention to my progress. I did, however, all I could from the first of January till the first of March, 1859, in applying myself to the intricacies of the law, hoping to be admitted to practice the first Monday of March, when the circuit court would be held. The time came, and both Finley and I applied for license. It was the custom then to appoint a committee of three lawyers to examine the applicants, and they were taken into a private room beyond the courthouse, and examined or not as the committee might choose, as the report was not then required to be sworn to. I remember very well the course which was pursued with reference to Finley and the writer of this. We were requested to meet the committee in the office of Bullard and Mitchener, which committee consisted of A. B. Bullard, B. L. Owen, and J. Robins. Bullard was asked to lead off in the examination, and being my friend and an old friend of my father and knowing that I had not been reading law long enough to stand an examination, he extended the kindness of his heart even beyond me over to my friend Finley and announced himself as satisfied. Owen was next called on, and having Finley in his office, and being especially fond of him, and his good sense and knowledge of the law teaching the same thing as to the deficience of his friend, took me under his protecting wing, and made the same announcement which Judge Bullard had just made. Colonel Robins, always the friend of the friendless, and the champion of all young men struggling for advancement whom he had reason to believe worthy, said if Bullard and Owen, with whom the young men had been studying, were satisfied, he ought to be and was. "But," said he, and I see the mischief twinkling in his eyes even now as I write after all these years, "young gentlemen, let me give you some advice. Be sure you have your fees secured. Have only three chairs in your office, one for yourself, one for your client, and one for your client's security," and he and the others gave that old time laugh that made the welkin ring and reported back to Judge Joel M. Acker, the then presiding Judge, that we were qualified and worthy of admittance to the bar. But I also remember very clearly they said, "Young gentlemen, you must write your own license." That was the first hard work I ever did in the law, but in some way I accomplished the feat in such way that the Judge signed it, and I supposed Finley did the same.

Now we were full fledged lawyers, but without practice and without means, and starting out in the midst of a strong bar. I remember at the term of the court at which we were admitted to the bar, Bullard and Mitchener and J. J. Lindsey were defending a man by the name of John Best on the charge of killing an old residenter, named Aycock, and they all recognized it as a kind of desperate case, and Bullard said to me, "you must make a speech in the case; it will be fine training for you." When the venire was drawn, my brother John was on it. When we came to pass on John, I told them he was a great law and order man, and if it was the kind of case he thought deserved hanging he would swing him up, but they said take him by all means on account of his relationship to you. But let me tell you the only thing that kept Best from hanging was because some body broke the old jail and turned him out; still I had an opportunity to make my maiden speech at the term at which I was admitted in an important case, which does not come to many lawyers.

November 3 & 17, 1905

After I came to the bar, and probably before, it was customary for the young lawyers to start out for different justice courts either

Friday evening or Saturday morning, each on horse back with two or more law books in his saddle bags, to attend to business wherein he had been employed or in such of business he hoped to get. But that was the extent of his effort. He placed himself on the ground where he could be seen and heard but he got no business unless those having it to give applied to him. It was as necessary for us to have saddlebags as it was for a physician, only ours were required to be larger, and made differently. I had been years at Tupelo before my old saddle-bags were worn out. The idea of taking a trip in a buggy then was never thought of when looking after a law suit in the country. We frequently kept the court and jury till after dark, and all the regular courts were held on Saturday. I remember very well the first case I was employed in. I got the case through the solicitation of old Jim Wright, a man from whom I was renting an office, and who was very well aware of the fact that he got no rent if I got no business. The case was before a justice of the peace, but instead of being in some old school house out in the hills, it was in the court house at Fulton, and my old precepter Judge A. B. Bullard was the opposition lawyer, instead of some of the boys I have mentioned. I succeeded in my case for a wonder, but one little incident of the trial has been fresh in my memory all these years. It was a case in which the evidence showed the woman against whom the suit was, owned all the property, and in speaking of her, for want of the knowledge of a better term, I said that which I had heard all through the years, "she is a free dealer." Judge Bullard after I had beaten him in the case, remarked to me by way of caution and admiration, "don't let me hear you use that expression again as long as you live," and I never have. You know it is often said in the country when a man has given all his property to his wife, "she is a free dealer." That's where I got the expression, but for a man to use the expression in a law proceeding was simply out of the question, and so it fell on Judge Bullard's legal ears.

We used to have some very interesting incidents to occur out in the country before the justice courts in my early days. I recall now an incident that occurred between Finley and me at old Smack some ten miles east of Fulton. It was in the spring or summer of 1859, soon after we began the practice of law, when neither Finley nor I was burdened with legal knowledge, but in this particular instance, I had this advantage of Finley. I went to the court knowing what I was seeking, and had prepared myself in the case, and had carefully written out a plea in abatement, and in those olden days such a plea was none too short, after putting in all the requirements of Coke and Blackstone; and so when the instrument was presented to the court and counsel it had a rather formidable appearance. The court had doubtless never seen such a plea, and it was rather a stunner to Finley also, but he was fine on retort and burlesque and ridicule. He picked up the plea very delicately, holding it high up between the fingers of one hand, with the other hand raised rather deprecatingly, turned the paper up and down, round and over several times, looked wise, and at the same time incredulous that such a document should be offered in that court, and with a kind of blow from his lips he called out, "what is this thing? What do you call it? Name it. Name this child." The effect was what might have been expected. The Justice of the Peace, supposing Finley really did not know what it was, and that as the lawyer did not know what it was, he was not supposed to be wiser than the attorney, and being on the Plaintiff's side any way, he brought one sweep of his hand and swiped the paper out of his court, and continued the case that I might have time to prepare something the court and counsel could comprehend. Finley laughed at me no little about the manner in which he disposed of my plea in abatement without making an argument, and often down through the receding years, I have enjoyed hearing him tell the incident.

NOTES

[1] Oliver Goldsmith's "Deserted Village."
[2] Fulton.
[3] Like other teachers of the period, Clayton was attempting to establish a school by getting a certain number of subscribers.
[4] Alabama.

CHAPTER III

The Bench, The Stump, The Circuit
MEN OF MISSISSIPPI
1859–1870

. . . I now think back on the years of the long ago at old Fulton, and the many men and women I have known there rise up before me in visions. . . .

THESE CHARACTER SKETCHES show Clayton at his best. Transporting us to the Southern community of more than a century ago, he describes friends and acquaintances of the "olden time" with clarity, humor, and affection and invites us to smile with him at these heroes with human foibles. Perhaps his greatest talent, however, lies in his ability to delineate character through a series of action-packed, often humorous anecdotes. Clayton's preachers raise their listeners "up in their seats" with fiery sermons. His politicians craftily attempt to get their opponents drunk before a big speech on the stump. Merchants outsmart Yankee cotton dealers. Shrewd lawyers—most notably Reuben Davis—manipulate judge and jury with audacious wrangling and clever legal tricks.

It is in these vivid personal portraits that we see most clearly both the individualism and the commitment to community of the white Southern male before and after the Civil War. If Clayton tends to accent positive attributes in his character sketches and ignores the

*contributions to the Southern community of blacks and women, it
must be remembered that he too was a product of that community
and its rigid structure. Although Clayton does not lament the past
here to the extent that he does elsewhere, this group of "Pen Pictures" perhaps summons the realistic Southern past most vividly—
simply by calling forth its people. It is in their individual portraits
that we can see the day-to-day realities of life in the "olden time"—
as they lived it, as we imagine we might have.*

OLD FULTON

February 2, 1906

When time has rolled its years on for forty-seven seasons, and
those who have lived all the way through and seen and realized all
the changes look backward and view the times then and now, they
almost always incline to the good old times of the long ago. To a
man who lived in Fulton from 1859 to 1861, the difference in the
then and now is very marked.

I have thought in looking back over the scenes of the long ago,
and measuring the bliss of the people of those olden days, that
probably those who have seen the prosperity and happiness of former times when they were full of youth, vigor and hope, in looking
back, look through partial glasses. But there is one thought which
has come and gone, and that is that the happiest and most contented
people in the world are those of the rural districts, in which I
include those residing in villages. In such districts and villages
everyone knows the wants and sorrows of all the others. If any fall
sick, or death touches a household, or sorrow of any kind overtakes
anyone, all the others know it, and are ready with a helping hand to
do whatever may be done to relieve the situation, while in a city, or
in our larger towns, men and women sicken and die, and the funeral
cortege passes our doors. I like the thought of sympathy and help.
The nearer neighbors and friends get together in loving sympathy
and helpful aid in time of trouble and sorrow, the nearer do approach the loving heart of the Man of Galilee, who never turned
anyone away empty who applied for help, and who wept with those

who wept. Thus it was in the olden time with the people who lived at Old Fulton, and each had a special interest in all the others, and the sorrow which touched one home had a sympathetic chord reaching to all the households in the old town; when death, with its gloom and anguish, overshadowed some neighbor, all the others felt the keen pang, and were ready to come in with muffled tread, to be a solace to the stricken ones, and when misfortune overtook some poor unfortunate man or woman, the whole town came to their relief.

The social intercourse of the people of that old town in the long ago often took the form of barbecue picnics. The river bottom was near to the town, near enough for all to walk, was well stocked with squirrels and some turkeys, and the river and Cumming's Creek were well supplied with fish, and the citizens would turn out en masse, the women, boys and girls with fishing tackle, and the men with their guns. Some would supply some old and trusty slaves, both men and women, to attend to the preparations of the dinner, the meats to be barbecued from the slain of the hunt. The men would divide up into equal companies for the day's hunt, and those who understood the habits of the squirrel would be on the ground ready to begin the work of the day by daylight. I remember one of these picnic barbecue hunts in which Captain Betts killed twenty-seven squirrels with a rifle, and Captain Keyes forty with a double barrelled shot gun, by eleven o'clock in the morning, that being the time we were to cease hunting. We had one hundred and eighty-one squirrels barbecued that day, and they, with the other viands we that day enjoyed, were enough to have satisfied the appetite of a king. But the sweet and pleasant intercourse of friend with friend, modulated and refined by the presence of our wives and daughters, was the chief charm of the occasion. From the time we all came in from the hunt, with nothing to do but to see that the old darkey cooks made no mistakes in the culinary department, until the October sun, with its gold and glory, began sinking rapidly towards the western horizon, we had nothing to disturb the joy of the occasion. And he who was prepared to enjoy nature at her best, and whose heart was susceptible to female charms, was surely blessed that

47

afternoon. But time brings her sorrows and disappointments. I know of but two men and three women of that happy little band who survive. One by one, like leaves of the forest before the zephyrs of fall, they have fallen and settled themselves down, "where the wicked cease from troubling and the weary are at rest." Shall not some of us look for the footfalls of these dear ones some good day, and hope to hear a welcome home?

March 2, 1906

Now, I will turn to speak some things in general terms and in a general way about some of the men and boys of old Fulton in the long ago. Fishing and hunting was a favorite pastime with the men in those olden times, and if I had recorded the many incidents which came under my observation and which I heard from those with whom I associated I could fill a book. I remember a little incident which occurred with Egbert Betts and a rabbit which deserves recitation. Egbert Betts and Bill Gaither had been out on a long jaunt fishing and were walking along home after the day's sport was over, tired and leg weary, and Egbert, to assist the foot with the hand, had cut him a walking stick of ordinary size and was using it for that purpose, when a rabbit scudded off before him and almost from under his feet. Under the impulse of the moment, and not with any expectation of hitting, and no thought of killing the cotton tail, he dashed his improvised walking stick after it, and to his and Gaither's astonishment, the hare stopped suddenly as if killed. On going up they found that the stick had entered between the leader and the bone of hind leg and stopped the locomotive power of the animal. When they looked at it and saw that the stick which had entered the leg was many times larger than the leg itself, Egbert said, "Bill, I will carry this rabbit and this stick just as it is up for exhibition to the boys because if we were to go up to town and tell them how it occurred without this demonstration, no set of men on earth would believe us." So the rabbit with the large walking stick still in the leg was carried up to town, and I myself saw it and heard their explanation of how it occurred.

Fox and deer hunting, driving, was also practiced. Some comical things sometimes occurred in connection therewith. One night we were out some three miles from home trailing a fox. We had talked so much of the pleasures of the chase that Shelt Stribling concluded he would try his hand in the chase with us. That night we had a warm trail for quite a distance, and I had kept right with the dogs until the fox was jumped, or flushed, and then we had a fine chase for about three or four hours, having about twenty-five dogs in the pack, and any lover of the chase knows what music they make. Occasionally we could see old Reynard, running like he was on wings just skimming the ground. When we had been in the chase about two hours, and when the interesting point of the chase was drawing on, Stribling and I came to a place in the by road which he recognized. It was then about eleven o'clock at night, and Strib thought he had enough, and in the midst of the thickest of the contest, he abandoned us and went home never to return to the fox hunt again.

One night we went out several miles east of Fulton, jumped a fox, chased him in fine style for several hours, then lost him altogether and made for home. When we got about the eastern suburbs of the town, our pack started another or the same fox, ran him into town and chased him through many of the yards, arousing the sleepers from their pleasant dreams by our fox hunters' yells, if any of you know what that means. Women thrust their heads out of the windows and joined in the hallowing, while the men left their beds and joined in the chase on foot, and some of them were at the stringing of the fox, which took place right in the midst of the town. Sometimes a fox will take a straight shoot right along a road for many miles with the hope of eluding his pursuers by that means, and the riders often get thrown off their guard, not expecting such a move, and are left behind. I remember such an incident on a fox hunt at old Fulton in which the fox took such a course and moved off seven miles in a strait course and left all the hunters behind except Ab Betts and me. We followed close as we could and got in at the stringing of old Reynard, while all the others had been at home for hours. When we caught the fox I told Ab unless we carried the fox or its tail, the boys who had been disappointed would never believe our tale. So Ab said, "Then I'll carry the whole fox," which he did to the astonishment of the other fellows, they having decided that the dogs had jumped a deer and run him off over to Bull Mountain. Our dogs were very fine on deer trailing. Sometimes they would be gone for several days and then come home with a small part of the foot of a deer tied to the neck of one of the pack with a note attached stating who killed the deer before them, and where, or how they were found with the deer, having themselves run it down. One time a note of the kind came to us from on Twenty Mile, showing that the deer had been killed over twenty miles from where they started it, and they still in hot pursuit. It was a magnificent pack; but those days are gone, and where are the hunters? Echo answers, where? It will not be long until those of us who remain shall hear the call, "Come ye too. Ye have served your time." Shall we be ready?

DOCTORS

September 1, 1905

In the olden time, long, long ago, on the banks of the beautiful named Indian stream, Mantachie, there lived an old country doctor, and these Pen Pictures would be lacking in completeness unless his picture is given at least a touch or two of the pen. He was a man of ordinary height, say five feet, ten inches, having a large bald head, high forehead, twinkling black eyes, a head full of sense, and a mind well stored with medical knowledge, a full-lipped mouth and—a silent tongue. The doctor never rode a well kept, fat horse, but almost always rode an old sorrel or bay horse, whose hip bones stuck out like the cheek bones of an Indian, whose ribs were prominent and whose eyes were sunken. The doctor was never in a hurry, and even if he had been, it is very likely that the horse could not have been aware of it. He was very careless in relation to his personal appearance and of his clothing, ordinarily wearing home spun and home made both winter and summer, and often the socks and pants seemed to have no affinity for each other. And when the doctor mounted his old sorrel horse on an old saddle, worn to a frazzle years ago, with stirrups and stirrup leathers of different kinds, and frequently tied together with two strings, with old brogan shoes, one tied and the other not, or with boots, with one leg in and the other out of the pants, wearing his home spun and home made clothing from hat to shoes, and the horse with hips high and dry and his ribs shining like walking sticks, and the breeze fanning his scattering hairs and his straggling form, and we have a picture that puts me in mind of Don Quixote de la Mancha, the wonderful knight errant of the middle ages, or Ichabod Crane, the school teacher of "Sleepy Hollow." But the doctor, notwithstanding his weird and ragged appearance, was a man of standing and reputation in his profession. Billie Keyes, now of Tupelo, but formerly of old Fulton, and probably a few more of the old residents will at once say, "That's Dr. Moore."[1] Well, that is true, and I will now proceed to give some of his additional peculiarities. He seemed more averse to talking than any man I ever knew. It was against his religion, so to speak, to give any information to a patient in relation to the remedies applied or the medicine given. Being called to see the child of a good old dame, but one who had a full share of inquisitiveness, while he was giving medicine to her child, she said to him, "Doctor, what kind of medicine is that you are giving my child?" "Pills," said the doctor. "But what sort of pills?" said the good woman. "Round pills," replied Dr. Moore.

At another time the doctor visited a patient in the country where they had the old puncheon floor, of which I have written heretofore, and being desirous of getting a spoon to use in giving medicine, and not wishing to ask for it, he knelt down on the floor and began raising up one of the puncheons. At this the good lady of the house said, "Doctor, what in the world are you looking for?" With a peculiar yawn which cannot be reproduced in writing, and which he used in all such circumstances, the doctor replied, "I thought maybe you had dropped a spoon down through the crack in the floor, and I am looking for it."

As I have said it was very much against Dr. Moore's inclination to hurry in going to see a patient, and if urged to do so, he would say, "Well, if he is that sick, he will die before I get there anyway."

At one time, however, a gentleman went for the doctor and was so persistent that he should make time on account of the critical condition of his wife, that he actually pressed the doctor into a canter on his old sorrel. But after moving on in that way for a time, he discovered that he had dropped his saddle bags containing his stock of medicine. "There," said the doctor, "that comes of making haste." There was nothing to do but retrace his steps till he found his saddle bags and medicine. When he found them, however, the bottles were much broken and the medicine scattered. The doctor gathered them all up together, remarking, "Ah, they have to be mixed anyway before they can be given," and then took his usual gait toward his patient's house, and that was the last time he was ever known to be pushed into a hurry.

Dr. Moore was much in demand as a consulting physician, and this was especially true of Dr. Mitchener's patients, a physician residing at Mooreville, whenever he needed counsel at all. Mitchener[2] was a much younger man than Moore, and had all confidence in him, and liked him very much personally besides. At one time Dr. Moore, together with two other doctors, were called in by Dr. Mitchener to consult about an important case. Having examined the patient, and retired from consultation, Mitchener asked at once for an expression from the attending physicians. Dr. Moore, thinking Mitchener was moving too rapidly in the premises, said to him, "Well, you are the Solomon of the occasion, suppose you give your opinion first."

A doctor will be sick as well as common mortals, and so Dr. Mitchener had the misfortune to languish on a sick bed, being very low in fact. So among other physicians he sent for his old friend and stand by, Dr. Moore. When Dr. Moore came in he did not go to the bed at once and examine the condition of Dr. Mitchener, and rush out a prescription in double-quick time, but, as his custom was, said nothing, and did nothing for quite awhile, except to give side view glances at the patient, but taking in all the situation all the same. Finally the doctor's wife could stand the strain no longer, and called out in much anxiety and trouble, "Dr. Moore, please examine my husband and give him something or he will die." Dr. Moore, in that inimitable manner, which no pen can picture, replied, "Madam, if he does, I'll take care of you." I have heard Dr. Mitchener tell this incident and laugh till his sides shook.

February 16, 1906

In going to Fulton occasionally before I moved there in 1859, I remember to have seen Dr. A. J. McWilliams, and probably was introduced to him. He had been before then rather prominent in politics, having been elected to the State Senate and served a term before 1855, and his reputation as a physician was as extensive as that of any in north Mississippi at the time. He was raised in north Alabama, near Athens, and received his training as a physician in the office of a local practitioner in Athens, never having attended a medical school.

Dr. McWilliams settled first at Old Van Buren, on the river, some fifteen miles south of Fulton, and remained there a few years, and then moved to Fulton, where he remained until he settled in Tupelo. In Dr. McWilliams' early manhood, he was a fine looking specimen of humanity, and possessed all the suave and bonhomie of a most delightful companion. He was known far and wide, throughout Itawamba and adjoining counties of Mississippi and the western counties of Alabama, where his practice was extensive, though over twenty miles from his home. While the Doctor was at one time in the early fifties elected to the State Senate and many years thereafter treasurer of his county, his real life work was that of administering to the sick, distressed and dying. No man ever called on Dr. McWilliams for help when sick that he didn't attend the call, whether rich or poor, bond or fee, and his smile in the sick room was worth many doses of medicine, however well administered. Dr. McWilliams was a man of about five feet eleven inches in height, having a magnificent physique, an iron constitution, a fine worker, never too tired to go again if sickness demanded, a great lover of his profession, always keeping well up with everything new in his line, a great reader of medical journals and books. He had a big head full of brains, and a heart as large as all out of doors, and a manner that won friends whenever they knew him. When he walked into a sick room and began examining the patient, confidence was assured at once.

I never knew a man having better judgement of good horses and never knew him to be without a good one longer than necessary to procure another after losing the one in hand. He had a horse which he drove and rode for many years at Fulton, called Leech, and which I have known him to drive seventy-five miles in one day and night in his practice, and I suppose he saw probably twenty patients during the time and administered to their wants.

The Bob horse which he owned when he moved from Fulton to Tupelo and which he used regularly for about eighteen years was bought for him by W. M. Gaither, of Fulton, and Dr. Mc never knew what he cost. He had done Gaither's practice for many years and had never asked him for pay, and so when Gaither had been appointed county treasurer of Itawamba and gotten in better shape financially than usual, he concluded to take a trip into Tennessee where he was raised and Dr. Mc asked Bill to bring him back a saddle and buggy horse and he brought him Bob. When McWilliams asked the price of the horse Gaither made some reply not to the point, and Dr. Mc himself told me he was never able to get out of him what the horse cost. But Gaither told me one day when I was talking to him that Bob cost him $250.00 and that he had never told Dr. Mc what he paid for the horse. The Doctor knew better than most men how to care for a horse, and had a fine knack at training the boys properly in that way who cared for his horses, both white and colored.

For the pure love of his profession, Dr. McWilliams was unexcelled, not that he loved it for the money which it brought him, but for the sake of the profession itself and the good he was thereby enabled to do for suffering humanity. The night never got too dark nor the weather too stormy or cold for him. He one time made a long trip over into Alabama in such cold weather that when he arrived at the home of the patient he was so near frozen to death he had to be lifted from his horse and carried into the fire and warmed up before he was capable of administering medicine. Dr. Mc enjoyed a good joke as well as any man you ever saw, and would tell one on himself as well as on others. He was very much afraid of snakes and it made no difference with him whether the snake was poisonous or not, they were all poisonous to him. I remember hearing him give his experience about running over some snakes with his buggy while out north of Fulton on a visit to some patients. He was driving along at a rapid trot with old George, when all at once he noticed a snake winding up about the wheel of his buggy and approaching dangerously near his feet, and he was thinking seriously how and where he should jump from the buggy if the snake should be whisked up around his feet, and about the time he was congratulating himself that the snake had been thrown off, he ran over and caught up on the wheels two or three more large ones, and this time they were jerked up into the buggy and fell around the Doctor's feet. Without any hesitation whatever, he dropped his lines over the splatter board and jumped laterally from the buggy saying, "here, Lord, take me as I am!" When the horse learned his master, of whom he was very fond, had left him alone, he pulled up and the Doctor reconnoitered carefully and cautiously, and learning their snakeships had vacated the buggy, he again took possession and went his way, thankful for his life preserved unhoped from perils seen and perils felt!

One incident in Dr. Mc's life I now recall that shows his disinterested friendship. J. W. Keyes, whom he knew from infancy at old Fulton, was taken sick with typho-malarial fever at Durrent, Mississippi, and his father, Captain Keyes, applied to Dr. Mc to go there and wait on him and bring him home if possible. He went, brought the young man to his own home in Tupelo, kept him for quite a while, and made no extra charge whatever therefor. When the last day shall come, I feel sure many will rise up and call him blessed, and he himself will hear the welcome plaudit, "Well done, good and faithful servant." I had rather have my name enshrined in the hearts of the people, as his is, than to possess the silver of Peru or the gold of Golconda.

LAWYERS

December 8, 1905, and January 12 & 19, 1906

I wish now to write of some lawyers of old Fulton, who were in full practice when it moved there in 1859. When I came to the bar, Russell O. Beene was district attorney for this district, and then as now included Itawamba county. He was then a man of mature age, I would say about fifty years old. He was at one time circuit clerk; he could and did carry all the papers in the office in his hat. It may seem somewhat strange to most of our readers to hear about carrying papers or anything else in one's hat. But it used to be very common for men to carry papers, or money, and often customary in the long ago to carry a handkerchief in the hat. You would say at once, "why, he would be dropping whatever he had in his hat out every time he took off his beaver." But you really should have seen one of those old fellows take off his hat. He was used to it, and it came like second nature to take hold of the hat with both hands, kinder bend the body forward, lifting it off the head as careful as if filled with eggs. I remember to have been working with my father by the road side when I was about fifteen years old, and I heard him say that morning he wanted to send about three hundred dollars that day to Pontotoc by the mail carrier to make a payment on his land. For many years an old man by the name of Mauldin had been carrying the mail between Pontotoc and Fulton, and we knew him well. In due time the old man came on, riding his old roan horse, and father stopped him and told him he wished him to carry the money for him, and to whom to deliver it. He very readily agreed to be my father's messenger, and I remember when father took the money out to give him, and offered to count the bills the old man said "no, put them in here" and taking off his old wool hat held it out for the money. Father handed up the money, however, to Mr. Mauldin and he very carefully smoothed out the bills, placed them in his hat, and taking hold of the hat with both hands, and bowing forward his bent form, as carefully placed the hat on his head and rode off. I said to myself, "will father ever get a return of that money?" But in due time the old man came by, took off his hat again in the same way and produced therefrom the land notes the money was sent to raise.

So you see in the olden time Russ Beene might have carried the circuit clerk's office in his hat, and especially if the hat should have been a high topped beaver, like I have seen him wear. Almost every one called R. O. Beene, Russ Beene; occasionally you would hear an old timer like old Uncle Jimmie Whitesides who called him Rush. I think Russell O. Beene was a Tennesseean. He was a man as full of the milk of human kindness as any one whom I have ever met. He came from the farm and never forgot his origin from the people, and was at one time, and for many years in fact, one of the most popular men in the office of circuit clerk and district attorney; he had been a member of the state senate before I ever knew him. He was of medium height, compactly built, hair almost white, even when a young man, sallow complexion, blue eyes, large head with unkempt hair and straight as an Indian. He was a man of wonderful memory. I never knew him to take a note of the evidence in any case, but he was very accurate in the presentation of facts. I have never known a man who was a better advocate than he. He was almost irresistable in summing up in his last speech to the jury. One advantage he had over many others was the fact that he always made his speech off hand, and never lost any time and interest looking after notes, and his training was so thorough in that respect that he carried the whole case in his mind and had the judgement to dwell on the strong points of a case. He was not an ignorant country man, though raised on a farm, but was really the best scholar of any of the lawyers at old Fulton when I went there, and could read Latin by heart as I can call off my letters.

Russ Beene had men in all parts of the country who would have fought for him as quickly as they would have defended their own wives. One of these was old uncle Jimmie Whitesides. I remember in 1856 that his friend "Rush Beene," as he called him, was running for district attorney against W. M. Inge of Corinth. One day Inge was making a speech at old Richmond, and said something about Beene which uncle Jimmie did not like, and he took out a long, sharp pointed knife and began picking his teeth with it, and said at the same time: "When you see old Jim Whitesides take out his knife and commence picking my teeth this way, you may know there are certain things in his mind about certain matters, now God bless you." And such men could be found then plentifully who would resent the least aspersion on his character. But the kindness of his heart was such, and the goodness of his nature so generally recognized that few men were even called upon to defend him. R. O. Beene was a splendid hand to turn incidents and happenings that came up at the spur of the moment to his advantage, or to the disadvantage of his adversary. When he and Colonel Inge were running for district attorney in 1856, they spoke together in Corinth, Colonel Inge's home. The speaking took place at a church, and while Inge was speaking, Beene took up the church Bible from the stand turned over Paul's first letter to the Corinthians to see if he couldn't find a text applicable to the occasion. So, when he rose to speak, he said: "My Corinthians brethren, I beseech you, by the name of our Lord Jesus Christ, that ye all speak the same thing, and that there be no divisions among you; but that you be perfectly joined together in the same mind and in the same judgement." The appropriateness of the text and sameness of names was such that the hit took well, and as a consequence, the brethren stood very firm to Russ at the polling day.

Beene unfortunately, like many of his day and generation would imbibe too freely some times. He himself said it would be a "mighty mean man that he would not drink with." Once when he was district attorney, and a very important murder trial was in progress, and he was to close the case the first thing in the morning, all the other attorneys having spoken the lawyers for the defense several in number, knowing his weakness in relation to liquor drinking, entered into conspiracy to drink him drunk by detail. The agreement was to get Beene in a crouse with them all and for them to drink lightly and only have a part of their number there at a time, while he would be on hand all the while. They succeeded so well as to keep him up all night, and they were all pretty full, but Beene, as they felt sure, was past making a speech that would be dangerous that morning. So, satisfied with the result of their efforts, they all separated after daylight. Russ staggered off to his room, and slept about an hour, got up and bathed his face and combed out his hair in good shape, and when court was called he walked into court, his adversaries and would-be destroyers watching to see the final effect of the night's potations, and believing still the impossibility of his making a successful speech. Beene had a way when he warmed up in making his speech in a case, of making a noise through his nose occasionally, which cannot be imitated in writing, but which was the very finest indication that he was going to make a magnificent speech. So, in a very short time after he began to make his closing argument, he began making these peculiar "nose grunts," and seemed never to have taken a drink, and he spread dismay into the ranks of his enemies one of whom remarked to the others, "Now we've played h——." It is said by those who heard him that morning that he made the speech of his life, and convicted the defendant.

Again, in the memorable campaign of the fall of 1855, in which Beene took a prominent part, his opponents thought Russ was too far gone to do them any damage. The candidate and other speakers stood behind a large oak log out under the forest trees, as a kind of table on which to place their books and papers, and when the time came for Beene to speak, he made a grab at the log, tore off some of the bark, kinder fell back, and then again came forward holding to the log for support, and finally steadied himself, and made the political speech of his life.

Before the war began Russell O. Beene had made a nice competency, and had bought him a plantation in the country, a little southeast of Baldwyn, had a fine lot of negroes to cultivate the land, and had himself moved on to it, but still attended the courts regularly and kept up active practice as a lawyer, being often retained in important civil suits, even while discharging the arduous duties of District Attorney. There was nothing on his place too good for the humblest man who might visit him. His laughter rang out all over the premises, and his smile and ready handshake were for all. He was unfortunate, however, in having so long been under the habit of drinking that it finally got the mastery of him; and in his old age, he was compelled to accept a small home in the Twenty Mile country of old Itawamba from his son and there he died at a good old age. But, if he had been prudent and careful, his old age might have been passed in as comfortable home as any the country afforded, and left a reasonable fortune for his family.

Pretty generally I have confined myself in these "Pen Pictures" to facts and incidents, hoping that my readers would remember that"History is Philosophy teaching by example." But, to the young men who have read my "Pen Pictures," I wish to say, there is no absolute safety except letting the vile stuff alone. The best men, most generous and noble hearted, will fall and do fall beneath his treacherous touch. Safety lies alone in "taste not, touch not, handle not the unclean thing." If anyone who reads this uses intoxicants as a beverage, and does not cease the use, remember when you are old and gray headed, and your bodies are racked with pain and anguish consequent on the poisonous effects of such use, I warned you faithfully.

January 19, 1906

Now, I turn to speak of a very dear friend, who had only preceded me some four or five years in admittance to the practice of the law at Fulton. Who can tell what the future has in store for young and hopeful hearts? And who can so far act the prophet as to be able to say this one of all the number will write the history of all our transactions? When we all began together in 1859, each full of life and hope, and whose horizons were flashed alike by bright anticipations of the coming years, who could guess that one of all the number would be telling of myself and all the others as they acted on the stage in the olden time—in the long ago? "Man proposes, but God disposes."⁵ We all walked and talked together in the long ago; surrounded by each other in our different places of meeting, we blessed the stars that brought us in contact, and really thought not of a historian of the band, nor of who should go or who survive. Yet, here I am now, sixty-nine years old this Christmas, solitary and alone of all the lawyers who were at the bar when I was admitted, writing, writing of the things that occurred, and of the men and measures I came in contact with in those olden days. Forty years from now who will Pen the Pictures? The fingers that now hold the pen with both hands as I write these lines, will soon drop from the pen and the tongue that so loves to talk to the friends and friends' friends of the olden time, will be silent forever on earth, and the warm hand grasp I enjoy so much, will relax its pressure, and the eye that so sparkles at the mirth of the old time friends will be glassy, and no more respond to the cheerful salutations that now greet me.

But I have not yet given you the name of the dear friend of whom I spoke above. His name was—yea, is still—Jasper N. Mitchener, and I now proceed to say something of him. He was raised on a farm, and moved to Fulton from near Mooreville, where his parents lived and died. He was man of rather slender build, ordinary height, coarse black hair, blue-gray eyes, beautifully fair, maiden-like cheeks, having a disposition equal to that of the loveliest woman. When occasion required, though, he was brave and chivalrous as the bravest. He was a fine office lawyer, arranging his papers nicely, and was a lawyer of strong judgement, and a fair practitioner, and in that respect improving all the while. When I went to Fulton in 1859 to study law, he was a partner of Judge Bullard.[6] In the beginning of 1861, he entered into partnership with J. J. Lindsey, and they practiced together about a year, but most of that time the Southland was a camp, and not much doing in the legal business. The South became a living camp, and all the young lawyers of old Fulton went off to the war, except Jappie. His health would not admit of his going. During the first two years of my residence at Fulton, Jasper Mitchener was as gay and full of vigor and work as any of the lawyers living there. In all the social amusements and gatherings he made a full hand, and enjoyed a good joke with the best of them. I remember having heard him tell his experience with a merchant there at Fulton by the name of Tom Bates, in relation to an application to borrow Uncle Tommie's pony. Jappie was like many other young men beginning life—quite poor. At the time of which I speak he did not own a horse, and in those olden times it was not thought beneath the dignity of a young man to borrow occasionally for a festive occasion. So the young men and women of the town, being invited out into the country for a social gathering of some kind, and the town being pretty well borrowed out, Jappie, as a last resort, thought of Uncle Tommie Bates' pony. In order to enjoy to its full the little incident, an acquaintance with our old friend, Bates, is necessary. He was a man of about fifty, sedate and somewhat self important, and had the reputation of being very close indeed. The boys used to say of him that a dollar never passed his hands without the scream of the eagle being heard. But with all he was kind hearted. It was with great difficulty, however, that he could make up his mind to lend anything which might be injured by the using. But Mitchener concluded he would try for the loan of the pony anyway. The pony himself was not attractive at all, being small and sleepy looking. Finally Jappie mustered the courage to approach Mr. Bates, and with many doubts and some hesitation made known his errand in relation to the loan of the pony. Uncle Tommie, raising his glasses to the top of his long, bald head, and looking in a kind of commiserative way, said: "Jappie, he would not carry you in the style you would wish to go."

When the young men began dropping into line for the wonderful conflict that was just in front of them, sadness and gloom touched Jappie's life because he could not go, too. His will was good, and his courage was equal to the occasion, but the hectic flush was upon his cheek, the hacking cough was disturbing his sleep, the wasting disease was taking his flesh, the sparkle of the eye was dimmed, the elasticity of his movements was gone, and hope of better things on earth had fled. So, to go to the tented field was impossible. What should he do? The father and mother were still living near old Andrews Chapel, then in old Itawamba, in a quiet country home, where peace and love and gentleness and grace reigned supreme, and there Jappie returned to their bosom, like the dove to the Ark, to quiet and rest. And while the cannon were sounding out death and destruction, ruin and desolation, where he could not mingle, he breathed his last quietly and peacefully and was laid to rest in that old graveyard near the old home to await the last message to the dead.

Jappie, I have rested by thy side many nights, and sat with thee round the cheerful fireside and listened to thy inspiring voice in the long, long ago; I have learned many legal truths from thy instruction and enjoyed many happy moments, both in business relations and social intercourse with thee. And now I write and you rest from your labors. Shall there not be another meeting—shall I not see that again—Who will say me nay? Not the voice of hope; not the longing after immortality; not the restless every outreaching mind; not the words of Holy Writ; but only the voice of doubt and distrust. But I will say to them, "Get thee hence, Satan, for thou shalt worship the Lord, thy God, and him only shalt thou serve."

November 17, 1905

Uncle Reuben Wiygle was justice of the peace at old Fulton when I came to the bar, and for many years thereafter. He was quite a character in many respects. He was very independent, knew no man nor set of men, and decided as his judgement and conscience dictated, and was very much adverse to any one questioning any thing he might do. In those days it was the usual thing to do to move to quash everything that was issued by a justice of the peace, and sometimes we had extended arguments, and read many authorities on such notions. J. J. Lindsey, being employed for the defendant in an attachment case before Esq. Wiygle, in which the justice himself had written out the papers, made a motion to quash the affidavit, and arose and with proper respect and decorum said, "If your Honor please, I move the court to quash the affidavit in this case." Uncle Reuben, without waiting for Lindsey to have time to give his reasons for the motion, promptly said, "no you don't, I wrote that affidavit myself, and I shall uphold it good or bad." Lindsey was smartly crestfallen, but the Justice ruled with a mailed hand and tolerated no dallying.

Reuben Wiygle kept the hotel at Fulton for many years, and was a great favorite with all who became acquainted with him, but before one became familiar with his manner, he frequently made them open their eyes in wonderment. For instance, if a stranger should ride up or drive up to the hotel and call for the proprietor, Uncle Reuben would appear, sometimes without shoes, sometimes with shoes, but having no socks. He was none of your palaver kind of landlords, but if you put up at his hotel you did it without solicitation. But often when even a stranger, who had never seen him before, applied for lodging for self and horse, he would say with the greatest seeming candor, but with an assumed gruffness, "get down and come in. I have nothing for your horse to eat, but plenty of good water for him to drink, and he can thrive on that." The stranger would scan him from head to foot trying to ascertain when he meant, but without avail. But before he left the hotel, he would become better acquainted with the peculiarities of mine host, and be ready to fall in with his ways.

Mr. Wiygle was one of the finest woodsmen I ever knew. He is the only man I ever knew whom you could not lose in Bigbee bottom. You might take him into the midst of the bottom anywhere, and he could come out the darkest night ever came. He was raised in Tennessee, but I do not know in what county. He was there with the Indians long before they left for the Indian Territory, and associated with them considerably, and liked them, and became quite familiar with them, and especially with the chief man among them. This Indian told Mr. Wiygle that his tribe had discovered and used a very fine silver mine there in the county and that they would show it to him if he wished it, but on condition he suffer them to blind fold him to carry him in and to bring him out, to which he readily agreed. Some distance from the mouth of the cave, but how far he was not able to tell, they put the bandages over his eyes and led him into the entrance of the silver mine, and when they had him fully within the cave, for such he designated it, they removed the blindfolds and then appeared to his astonished vision the most wonderful chance of silver that ever mortal man beheld. Silver in the rough, silver in bars, silver piled and silver scattered loose, and silver enclosed in the rock. They showed him their manner of disengaging it from the rock and their way of shaping it into bars, and other shapes. He remained in the cave with the Indians for several hours, and they again put the blindfolds upon his eyes and carried him out and quite a distance from the entrance before removing them, so that he was not able to locate the cave. Some time after this, the Indians were removed to the Indian Territory and with them the old man who was Wiygle's friend. Wiygle tried to get him to show him the mine before they were carried off, but the Indian said if he were to do so the other Indians would kill him. Wiygle after searching for quite a while after the Indians were removed, and making no discovery, gave up the search. After waiting some years he concluded to make a visit to his old friend in the Indian Territory to see if he could not induce him to return and show him the silver mine, and if not, then get such instructions as would enable him to find it. Mr. Wiygle threaded the pathless woods and forests alone and afoot from Tennessee to the Indian Territory, braving the danger of the wild beasts and wilder men, the floods and unknown wilds, and finally landed with the proper tribe and found his old friend; but no consideration could induce him to return to his haunts. But he was willing, and did give his friend such instructions as he felt sure would enable him to find the cave where the silver was. So armed with the information of his old Indian friend, he footed his way back over the long lonesome and weary road to the hills of his Tennessee home, and began search for that which he knew would make him rich, and which he felt confident of finding. He took none into his confidence, but tramped the silent woods for the silver cave for days and weeks without avail. One day, after he had become much discouraged and even almost despondent, he found, not that for which he was looking, but a hog carrying in its mouth a man's leg with a boot still on. This led him to think his own life might be endangered, and so he pulled up, and left off looking for the silver mine for all time to come, came to Mississippi, settled in Monroe county, and moved from there to Fulton, where he lived and died. He was a great reader of the Bible. You might go to the little old office just across the way from the hotel, and you were apt to find Uncle Reuben poring over his big family bible, lying open on a table before him.

January 26, 1906

When I was attending school at old Richmond, I used to pass by where J. D. Barton then lived in going to and from my father's and remember very well seeing Jim Barton, as we all called him, leaning back in the old fashioned split bottomed chair pouring over Coke and Blackstone. This was in 1855 and 1856, and I think Barton was admitted to the bar in the latter part of 1856, or the first part of 1857. He never moved to Fulton, but remained at his old home north of Richmond, and began the practice before the Justice of the Peace courts. He was considerably advanced in years when he was admitted to the bar, and had then a considerable family.

Barton was a tall angular man, lightly built, having long arms and fingers, with red hair and red complected. He was a man of some aspirations politically and in a judicial way. During the latter part of the war he offered for the legislature at the same time Jacob Braden was running for the same place. Jim Barton was always inclined to offer as a speaker, and he had a characteristic manner, and there was considerable fun in his make up. During this canvass with Braden, Jim made a hit that carried him to success in old Itawamba. "Gentlemen and fellow citizens," he would say, "do not get my name and that of my friend Braden mixed. I will state it this way; if you want to vote for me put in a ticket for Jim Barton, but if you want to vote for my honorable opponent, then vote Jake Braden. But if you cannot remember these names, and want to vote for me, then go for the Little Red'en; but if you want to advance the star of my honorable opponent, cast your suffrage for the Big Black'en!" Of course that raised the laugh, and attracted attention to both Barton and Braden, one of whom was a tall, but small red haired and red faced man, while the other was a heavy set two hundred and fifty pounder, and as dark a white man as you generally see.

The hit really cut both ways, and resulted in the election of both. After the war Barton moved to Saltillo, and entered into partnership with General Finley,[7] who then and for many years thereafter, lived in Guntown. They did a very considerable practice, and Barton was a conspicuous figure in the courts for a good many years. He was somewhat peculiar, having the most unbounded confidence in all judges and chancellors, and was never known to give them any trouble. Until a judge or chancellor decided against him, he would contend strenuously, but when they decided against him, he bowed in humble submission to the ruling, and was never known to say any word of criticism, not even the implied criticism of saying "we take an appeal, your honor," or "we'll see what a higher court will say."

He was really the most deferential toward those in authority of any lawyer whom I have ever seen at the bar. He had a kind heart, and there was also a streak of dry humor in his make up, and often you could scarcely determine whether he was in cold earnest, or used irony. I remember to have been engaged in a case in opposition to Major Barton once before chancellor Whitfield,[8] in which Whitfield did not know how to take him. It was a case involving a question of trust. Barton had all his evidence in, but claimed not to be ready for the hearing on account of having lost his Brief. He said to the chancellor, "If your Honor please, I have lost my Brief; that is I have lost that part of my Brief which I have made. It was only in part completed, but I have lost that and cannot well proceed with the case." The chancellor told him that he did not think the excuse sufficient, and that he must proceed with the case. When it came to Barton's turn to address the court, he proceeded to a discussion of trusts in general. The chancellor stopped him and said, "Mr. Barton, do you contend this is a case of express trust or implied trust?" "If your Honor please," replied Barton, "I shall first contend that it is an express trust, and if I find I am wrong in that, then I shall claim that it is an implied trust."

A little further on with the case he picked up a law book, Story's *Equity Jurisprudence*, and turned to the chapter on trusts, which was over one hundred pages long, and said to the court, "If your Honor please, I will begin reading here on trusts and if I find anything which I think applicable, I will call your Honor's special attention to it," at which chancellor Whitfield broke in with the surprise and deprecated expression. "Mr. Barton, are you going to read the whole chapter on trusts?" Finally we got through with the case, Barton in the meantime, having several times referred to his lost Brief. When the chancellor rendered his decision, which was adverse to Barton, he was on his feet at once, saying, "If your Honor please, as I said before, my Brief was not a completed brief, but I desire to say so far as I had gotten with it, it was in accordance with your Honor's decision." The chancellor did not know how to take Barton, and called me round to the Bench and asked me what Barton meant, thinking he might be poking fun at him.

March 2, 1906

I think God knew what was best for man when he gave the command to "multiply and replenish the earth." I am led to make this remark on thinking of an old bachelor whom I knew at Fulton, and remembering his sad end. His name was Coleman Robinson. He was well educated, his father being considered rich in those days, and after completing his education in school he studied law, obtained license to practice, set up an office in Fulton, had a fine library of law books and many literary works besides, and was himself a great reader. He had left his office at Fulton when I came to the bar, and gone back to his father's old home in the country some fifteen miles southwest of town, he having inherited the old homestead and a goodly number of slaves.

There was no end to his reading, and he seemed to be as anxious to succeed at law as any of us, but he had absolutely no applicable capacity. He could not manage a case in court. You know it is often said of those lawyers who say but little in the court, but manage business well outside and write up their papers correctly, "they are good judges of the law but are not good pleaders."

That's what many people call public speaking at the bar. I heard this said of Coleman Robinson once and I repeated the remark to Duke Shelley,⁹ and Duke's reply was, "Well if he knows it, it is about in him in lumps undigested." Coleman finally quite holding himself out as a lawyer, and was elected as county surveyor, and did considerable work as such for several years. He was a failure financially, and many suits were filed against him both in the justice courts and the circuit court, and he always appeared as his own lawyer, and made the best defense he could. Not long after the war, we had a county court, presided over by the probate judge and two justices of the peace, and had a court once each month. Among other provisions of the county court law was one that when you took an appeal from a justice court you took it to the county court, and after it was tried there you took it to the circuit court if you wished to go further with it. In one of the cases which was brought against Coleman Robinson before a justice of the peace, not being satisfied with the decision of the justice, he appealed directly to the circuit court, ignoring the county court altogether. When circuit court convened, the plaintiff moved to dismiss the appeal because it had been taken to the wrong court. The judge asked Mr. Robinson what answer he had to make to the suggestion that he was in the wrong pew; Coleman arose, long, slim and gaunt, and said, "If your honor please, I paid no attention to the county court, but considered it an interloper!" Of course he went out of court, a wiser, if not a richer man.

Having read and seen much of literature, and noticed how the people admired the poetry of Buck Owen,[10] Coleman concluded to try his hand with the muse. So after carefully conning over and re-writing several times, he had two lines which he thought would do to submit for criticism. So he carried them to Buck Owen, the prose poem writer as well as a real poet, both of rhyme and blank verses, and submitted them for his judgement. When Owen looked them over here is what he found. "As she slips she slides along. A trusty friend is hard to find!"

Well really, how much better poetry could some of us write if we were put to the test?

When Coleman Robinson had passed the middle of life he had lost everything he inherited from his father, and went and lived with a colored man named George Burnett the rest of his life, and George cared for him as well as he was able as long as he lived. George had married one of the Robinson slaves, tho he himself was free during slave times. We all called him free George, and he was raised by an old gentleman by the name of Moore,[11] and for whom Mooresville was named and we all knew him as "Hatter Moore," as he was a hatter by trade. I never knew George's history, how he became free and etc. but he surely acted nobly by Robinson.

April 13, 1906

In the present article I shall speak of some of the lawyers who used to visit Fulton at the time I began the practice of law. It was the custom then for certain prominent lawyers of Aberdeen, Pontotoc and Jacinto to attend regularly on the circuit courts at Fulton, and occasionally one came from Columbus, Ripley and Houston. The journey was made on stage, in buggies, or on horseback. I remember to have seen both General Davis and General Gholson[11] come into Fulton on horseback from Aberdeen immediately after the courts opened up after the close of the war.

The first one of these lawyers about whom I shall write is General Reuben Davis, and of him I will doubtless have more to say than any of the others, for he was the great criminal lawyer of Mississippi, and always for the defense.[13] He was a tall man, somewhat round shouldered, large bald head, prominent nose, and I think the most piercing gray eyes I have ever seen on human face. He was not a classically educated man, but had a good English education. He was educated for a physician, and practiced for a short hand, and his first wife called him "Doc" to the day of her death. Hoping to do better at law than at medicine, he perused Kent and Blackstone and Wharton, and was admitted to the bar. The court house in Monroe county in those early days was at Quincy,[14] and there General Davis, but who was not then a General, owned a log cabin for his home, and his wife cooked his meals, and he himself said to me those were really the happiest days of his married life. Soon the court house was moved to Aberdeen, and having accumulated a large amount of money by his practice, he built himself a fine old fashioned house something over a mile from the city of Aberdeen, where he lived till the time of his death, at about eighty-five years.

General Davis was the most splendid criminal lawyer in his palmiest days of any it has been my fortune to have known. From as far back as 1846 I knew of him as always being retained for the defense in all important murder trials. He refused to prosecute any man in those days, and up to the time he lost prestige on account of his age. He was a fine judge of men, and never forgot anything he had ever learned of men or things. He could come as near choosing the right man in the right place, and made as few mistakes in the management of a case as any lawyer I have ever noticed. He had a knack of placing the evidence in a case before the jury in the most favourable way, and seemed to know just when to stop questioning a witness. When he appeared before a jury to argue the case, his manner always indicated that he felt the responsibility of having the life of a human being in his hands and whatever he thought necessary to be said and the manner in which it should be said, was done. I have seen him talk to the jury for hours with the tears dropping off of each cheek as he walked back and forth before them. It used to be said even by lawyers that General Davis was a fine criminal lawyer, but that he was deficient in the civil law. My estimate of him, however, is different. It is true he had more criminal than civil cases; but Reuben Davis was a man of big brain, a fine all round lawyer, and when he placed his mind and thought on any case thoroughly, he came as near going to the bottom of it as most men. But his special tact was in judging jurors and in placing before jurors in the most advantageous light the evidence in the cause and then in his weird and canny way of holding up the case before the jury. I knew very much of General Davis and saw him often before I met him at the bar. I remember of him as far back as 1847 or 1848, in the trial of the case of Scaggs on a charge of the murder of Lenas Smith. The killing took place in 1846 at Scaggs' house, and if Scaggs and his wife had been competent witnesses then as now there would never have been any trouble in Scaggs securing his acquittal; but as it was then, there were two trials, and in the first Scaggs was found guilty of manslaughter, and sentenced to the penitentiary for twenty-five years. The case being reversed by the Supreme court, Scaggs was put on his trial the second time and acquitted. In this last trial, Davis, who fully believed in the innocence of Scaggs, had a strong struggle for his client's liberty and used some strategem that bordered well nigh onto contempt of court.

Hugh R. Miller was judge of the court at the time, and rather a dangerous man to play with on the bench. Mrs. Scaggs, wife of the prisoner, had taken out a warrant for the arrest of Smith the deceased, only a few days before the killing, but which had not been served when the killing took place. This warrant Davis offered to read to the jury, but Miller told him it was not competent. "But," said Davis, "if your honor please, I wish to read it to your honor before you rule on it." The judge told him that was not necessary. The truth is, Davis wished the jury to hear it read, it not being the custom then as now to send out the jury while discussing the propriety of permitting certain evidence to go to the jury, but they remained and heard what was proposed to be introduced and the reason given pro and con. So Davis said again, "But your Honor cannot tell whether this paper is competent or not unless you hear it, and I propose to read it to your Honor." I suppose Judge Miller thought the easiest and quickest way out of the matter was to let the General read the document, and then at once, without any argument, rule that it was not competent, and this he did with considerable vehemence. But Davis, with that firm set expression on his face which he so often assumed, mingled with a smile of contentment, remarked, sotto voce, "get the effect from the jury if you can." When the General was arguing the case, and come to speak of this paper, Judge Miller would stop him as soon as possible; but frequently during the argument Davis went like a cyclone at the paper, and would linger about it as long as he could without going to jail for contempt. Finally he said "gentlemen of the jury, if a man were to treat my wife as Smith did Scaggs' I'd kill him. I'd cut him to mince meat and throw him to the dogs and hold my ears to the ground to hear his first screams from hell!"

I remember another important murder trial in which General Davis was representing the defendant, and wherein he showed shrewd discernment. It was the case of William Standefer charged with killing a man named Barker. It was a bad case. Barker having been waylaid and shot, and the only question was did Standefer do it. There was an important witness for the state, an unsophisticated country man, whose testimony Davis was very anxious in some way to weaken or destroy. Everything was arranged for the trial on the next day, and the General was anxious and restless after supper, and walking around by Dr. McWilliams' office[15] for exercise, he

72

saw the doctor and a happy thought flashed into his mind, and he said, "Dr. McWilliams, are you specially busy this evening?" "No," said the doctor. "I am at your service if you want anything, General." "Then come and walk with me," said Davis, and taking the doctor by the arm, walked around town with him for quite a while, and finally dropped into where this dangerous witness was. They saw there and talked with the witness for some time on general topics, and then had some words about what he knew about the Barker killing, but nothing particular. They then walked back to the doctor's office, and then General moved on to his hotel. Davis said not a word to Dr. McWilliams about taking note of what was said, and the doctor had no suspicion that he would be called as a witness. But next morning he was summoned as a witness for the defense. When this witness was examined by the state and turned over to the defendant for cross examination, Davis put on one of his fierce looks and said to the witness, "Sir, look right at me. Do you know me sir?" "No, sir," the witness meekly replied. "Did you ever see me before, sir?" "No sir," was the same reply. "Sir, didn't Dr. McWilliams and I have a talk with you last night about this case at the place where you were staying here in this town?" "No, sir, I had no conversation with either one of you and I never saw Dr. McWilliams in my life and never saw you before now." "Stand aside, sir," and that same satisfied and compressed smile touched the General's face. When the state closed its case, Dr. McWilliams, a man known to everybody to be possessed of the highest character and unflinching integrity, was placed on the stand and contradicted the state's most important witness, and broke the force of his testimony.

April 20, 1906

Passing back over the past, my memory fixes upon another trial in which I very well remember the skill exhibited by General Davis in the conduct of the defense of a man charged with murder. It was just after the war had closed, and for a killing which occurred during the war, and in August 1863. It was on the trial of Isaac Sullivan on the charge of murder for the killing of Dr. J. W. Mitchener at Mooresville.[16] I was employed to assist the District Attorney in the prosecution, and the skill of General Davis to which I refer above was in the cross examination of Mrs. Webb, a state's witness and wife of Jerome Webb. The killing took place only a few feet east of Sullivan's residence, in the town of Mooresville, and Webb lived only about fifty yards east of the Sullivan residence. Mitchener was passing the road, which ran in front of Sullivan's house, going west in his buggy, and consequently passed by the Webb residence. There were two young ladies on horseback just in the rear of Mitchener's buggy, but not near enough to see the killing. So Mrs. Webb was the nearest person to the parties when the killing took place, except Sullivan and his family. Mrs. Webb was sitting in her front door combing her hair when Mitchener passed, according to her statement, and she saw the Doctor pass, and he spoke to her and she to him, and soon thereafter the gun fired. They knew Mrs. Sullivan was going to swear that Dr. Mitchener attacked and abused Sullivan, and even got out of his buggy and drew a pistol on the defendant, and then got back in his buggy, and was shot by Sullivan in self defense. So you can see the importance to the defense in showing by Mrs. Webb that as much as five or ten minutes elapsed after Mitchener passed before the gun fired. Very few people have any conception of time. They will speak of a thing lasting five or ten minutes which passed in a few seconds. Davis, knowing this, and also having in mind the thought that Mrs. Sullivan was very much in need of some substantial corroboration, sought and obtained such corroboration in the cross examination of Mrs. Webb, by making her say that it was five to ten minutes after Dr. Mitchener passed before the gun fired. This was all he wanted, and he crossed her no more. If we had known the importance it was to the defense, I have no doubt that we might have held the watch for five minutes and she would have placed the time at less than a minute. When Davis had solicited from Mrs. Webb what he wanted, he seemed altogether unconcerned, and simply passed the witness out; but it was the grant point in the case, and the one in which he dwelt most in his speech to the jury, and which won him the case.

General Davis was not less a statesman than lawyer and jurist. He was in congress when his state passed the ordinance of secession, and had been for some time. I now recall a description given of him by a correspondent of the *National Intelligence* in 1860, in which he spoke of him as he sat in his seat in the House as having the appearance of "Shakespeare turned cotton planter," and I thought the penpicture a good one. General Davis was on the Supreme Court bench for a short while in the early forties, but which Court was then called the "High Court of Errors and Appeals." General Davis was elected District Attorney somewhere in the forties also, but the prosecution of criminals was so foreign to his nature that he resigned, and again enrolled himself on the side of the defense. The General was in command of the State's forces during the war, and in the fall of 1861, when a heavy force was called out for sixty days to assist the Confederates at Bowling Green, Kentucky.

After the Democrats regained power in our State in 1875, General Davis became very much disaffected toward his old party and party friends, and went over the Green Backers,[17] and finally the Republican party. With all Davis' good qualities, he was a man of considerable vanity and he could not see young men whom he and many of his friends and admirers considered his inferiors in ability promoted above him, and this led to his political action above mentioned.

In the last years of General Davis' life, he wrote and published a book, called *Recollections of Mississippi and Mississippians*, and in the sale of which he was engaged at the time of his death. It is really a very fine literary production. His experience and acquaintance with the early times of Mississippi and the leading men of the State was extensive, and he was engaged in many of the stirring events of the early times of the State, and the book is more readable than a romance. To all lovers of pure English prose composition the book has its charms. Ths history is written in good, plain English, and the events related bring their own pleasure to the reader by their naturalness. I recall now one short sentence in relation to his special friend, James T. Harrison, which I always thought most beautiful and charming. After speaking of Harrison for a considerable time, and then of his death, he closed with something like this: "Harrison, shall we not see each other again? Ah, Harrison, I shall meet thee again!" I remember to have been talking at one time to Colonel R. O. Reynolds of the English classic in which General Davis' book was written, and we both called attention at the same time to the beauty and charm of the above expression.

General Davis was from home in the interest of his book when his great soul was called away. My memory serves me now that he was at Huntsville, Alabama and that he was in his usual health, walked out from his hotel for refreshment, as was his habit, returned to his room and was found shortly thereafter on the bed dead. When we think of the stirring scenes through which he passed, the great surging flood-tide of passion which passed through his soul and mind, in his many conflicts, legal and political, and then come to look upon him calm and severe in death, we can but exclaim, "Man can do much; God can do all things!" Sleep, General. I trust that with all other things which you discovered during your long and eventful life, you failed not in the one thing needful. Every generation has its men and measures, and they differ from those of other generations. When we review the stirring scenes of the late thirties and early forties, and remember how different they were to the present, and in what that difference consists, we are constrained to decide in favor of our own times. But those early times were more favorable for producing orators than the present. Forensic eloquence is not now thought of, while then it was the chief thing. This is peculiarly a utilitarian age, while then men were more largely governed by sentiment and moved by eloquence. Young men of that olden time, when educated for some public position, generally had grander and more lofty ideals before them than now, and the rich and well-to-do were not raised in the midst of stocks and bonds and moneybags as is now the case with the rich, but they were then brought up in the fields and woods, dwelling much with nature, and breathing in her inspiring scenes. Such near contact with nature and nature's God were naturally inspiring and uplifting. Now, if a man has means he has to work hard to preserve and conserve the same, and it keeps his thoughts in a different and lower channel and the young man raised under such circumstances partakes more or less of the parental surroundings.

Now, it is stocks and bonds, money and mortgages, requiring special personal attention; then it was hounds and guns, poetry and romance.

May 11, 1906

General S. J. Gholson was a prominent figure in those olden times. When I first remember him, he was a Federal Judge, holding court at Pontotoc. He had a life job at a fine salary and an easy place, as the criminal business of that court was light before the war. Judge Gholson told me in a conversation I had with him since the war, that when he went on the bench he found that the planters from the Mississippi bottom had been for some years ignoring the process of the court when they were summoned as jurors, and his predecessor had been entering a fine of one hundred dollars against each of them, and they preferred paying that to serving as jurors. But when Judge Gholson learned the situation, he entered a fine of five hundred dollars, compelled them to pay it, and said that after that he had no trouble with them, and had as nice set of gentlemen for jurors as any judge could wish. When the war came on all Judge Gholson had to do to have a life tenure of his office was to have moved across the line north and waited for the close of the war, and in the meantime to have drawn his salary. The United States government would have been glad for such an opportunity. But no, Gholson was a true lover of his homeland, and resigned his position in the Federal service, and cast his lot with his country, and served her well and honorably till the last, carrying the balance of his life an empty sleeve, the left arm being amputated at the shoulder joint. Some may have doubted the capacity of General Gholson as a wise commander, but none ever doubted his loyalty to the cause of the South nor his courage in the presence of the enemy. After the war was over General Gholson was a regular attendant and practitioner at the Fulton bar. I remember at one court immediately after the war he and General Reuben Davis both rode horseback from Aberdeen to court at Fulton, and I happened to be at the hotel when they came in, and I know I was struck with the difference in the way they stood the trip, Davis being worn out and almost ready to go to bed, while Gholson was game to the bottom and gay as a fighting cock. He was a man of great powers of endurance. He was a very earnest practitioner of law, but he did not have the reputation for legal learning possessed by some of his compeers. He had a very warm heart towards his brethren of the bar, and was especially kind to young men just entering the profession, and ever ready to lend them a helping hand.

September 29, 1905

The first good view I ever had of Buck Owen was on the fourth of July, 1850, when I heard him deliver an oration at the ford of old Boguefalah, [18] a mile east of Mooreville, at which time we had a big barbecue and fourth of July celebration. The custom in those olden times was to meet specially to celebrate the natal day of our country, and the Declaration of Independence was read and an oration delivered in patriotic style, the people generally feasting on barbecued meats and other viands and enjoyed themselves wonderfully. I remember Buck Owens' appearance very well that day, and how he held his audience spell bound by his eloquence. He was a man of splendid physique, about five feet ten inches in height, massive head, well rounded, prominent forehead, large dark eyes, with dark beard and his gesticulation was as near perfect as that of any speaker whom I had ever seen or heard. From the time he made this speech in 1850 down to the time of his death I was acquainted with his movements. In 1853 he was elected to the lower branch of our State Legislature, and made a very faithful and capable member. I remember even now one question which was before that legislature and in which he took a prominent part, and made a very eloquent speech which was published in the papers at that time and which I thought very tender and touching. In those olden times before a saloon keeper could obtain license to retail liquors he had to get a majority of the legal voters in the town or territory in which he proposed to sell to sign a petition recommending him as a sober and suitable person to sell such liquors. In the legislature while

Buck Owen was there a proposition was made to so change the law that the same right of petition should be extended to all females over the age of eighteen, and unless a man proposing to retail could get a majority of all legal voters in the prescribed district and all females over eighteen, he was not allowed to carry on his business. On this bill Owen made a very fine speech in advocacy thereof, and painting the picture of the wife and mother in their sorrow, desolation and woe consequent on the use of intoxicants by the husband and father, and described the drunkard's wife with her wan cheek and wasted form and anxious hours and tear-dimmed face, and threw upon the canvass such a woe-begone picture of suffering and want and grief and sorrow and death, that came near sweeping the legislature off its feet.

When Buck Owen stood for re-election in the fall of 1858, politics had gotten to such a fever heat, the Know Nothing[19] craze having come in, and Owen being on that side of the question, he was defeated, notwithstanding there was nothing against him. In the meantime he had studied law and been admitted to the practice, and formed a partnership with his brother, B. L. Owen. I remember very well hearing him deliver an oration at the Fair Ground one half mile east of old Richmond in September, 1859. He was married then and his wife was sick, and he could only go hurriedly and make the speech and then was compelled to return to the bedside of his sick wife. The speech was a magnificent and even a magnetic one, in which he painted in glowing colors and brilliant language the advantages of the contented, happy life of the farming people, with their happy homes and lovely scenes; their broad acres or little cottage on the hillside, with the valley blooming in beauty in sight; the glad hearts of the wife and children, as the laborer wended his way up the flower-bedecked walk to meet them after the toil of the day was over, ready to lie down and dream of better things on the morrow; and then showed, in his inimitable way, that the hope of the perpetuity of our great country was in the virtue and intelligence of the common yeomanry of the country. There was a very fine audience, and it might be truly said that old Richmond and her vicinity had "gathered there her beauty and her chivalry," and among them many of Buck Owen's best and staunchest friends and associates, and they were very anxious for him to remain with them and enjoy the festivities of the occasion. But when he completed his speech he referred to the pressure made upon him by his friends to stay over during the other exercises of the Fair. "But," said he, "I hear a voice you cannot hear / That tells me not to stay; / I see a hand you cannot see / That beckons me away." With that he descended from the platform and hurried home to be with her who was the hope and joy of his life, then sick at old Fulton. I also heard him deliver a school oration at the close of our school in Mooreville that I think was a master-piece of oratory, and which was to have been published at the request of the school, but some drunken printer lost the manuscript and it was thus lost to the world.

Buck Owen delivered the fourth of July oration at old Camargo[10] in 1856. It was a very large gathering, many having come from Fulton and Richmond. The orator sustained his reputation of former years, and almost lifted the audience off their feet by his flights of eloquence, and such an ovation as he received after the speaking was over only comes to a man once in a lifetime. But I do not think I ever knew a man freer from vanity than he, or any one who received the compliments of his friends and admirers with more suave and placid demeanor. His cordial hand-shake, with the sparkle of those wonderfully lustrous eyes looking you square in the face was a benediction for days to come, and even clings to me through all these eventful years.

October 6, 1905

In 1853, when Buck Owen was making his first race for the legislature, the candidates were being introduced to the audience as their time came to speak, and when the time came for Owen to be introduced, he stepped forward and said: "Gentlemen and fellow citizens: I need no introduction. This is my home and you all know me and I know you. 'My foot's upon my native heath and my name's McGregor.'" Buck Owen was a great lover of Sir Walter Scott's writings, both prose and poetry, and often quoted snatches of the poems and incidents of his prose. In the long, long ago,

probably in the late forties or the early fifties, he made a trip to the
west in northwest Texas, and rode horseback over the beautiful and
lovely scenes furnished by that wonderful land, in what now consti-
tutes the heart of the cotton growing and wheat raising section of
the state, but which was then an almost unbroken landscape of grass
and flowers, with occasional strips of small timber festooned with
the grape and the muscadine; and the things which he there saw and
heard and took into his capacious memory, furnished themes and
incidents for illustrations in his orations to the day of his death.

Buck Owen was a poet, as well as a statesman and an orator. He
used to often print short poems in the Fulton *Herald*, sometimes
under the name of "Orion," or "Will o' the Wisp," or "Will," and
every lover of poetry was glad to see their appearance. He was very
foolish, as it is often termed, about his wife and children, and I
remember very well the poem he published on looking into the face
of his first born babe. He called it "Heart Whispers," and it was
written in blank verse, and I have always considered it a gem of the
first water. I give you the first half sentence of it:

> My sleeping Babe, sweet firstling of our Love,
> Thy gentle, doating Mother's love and mine.
> I gaze upon thy hush'd and happy sleep,
> And watch thy tiny arms, upraised, as if
> To welcome to thy breast the angel forms
> That bend above thy couch, whispering soft
> Celestial music to thy young spirit.

And then the prayer of safety against the fear the child might come
between them and their God comes like a Holy dove of hope:

> Sleep my child,
> And He, who knows how earnestly we ask
> That we suffer not thy sweet loved image
> To come between Him and us will guard thee,
> And keep thee safe from every earthly ill.

He also wrote a rather long poem, consisting of over a thousand
words, and called "The Chase." This was never published during
his lifetime, but I got the original manuscript from his daughter and

only surviving child and copied the same and had it published about a year ago in the daily Memphis *Commercial Appeal.* This poem is very much on the style of Scott's *Lady of the Lake,* and the local and historical incidents and scenes are well and beautifully described and to an old hunter, as I am, the sound of the horn and the music of the opening pack, so well and timely touched off in this poem, come to the ear like a thing of beauty and a joy forever.

In addition to these he published many idyls and short love ditties, which were charming. He also wrote very excellent prose poems, that is, prose compositions with so much of the ring and sweetness of poetry in them that we felt like classing them as poems. I remember one of these prose compositions which appeared in the Fulton *Herald* in 1859 or 1860, titled, "Look on this Picture Then on That," which I always believed one of his finest productions, and in which he painted the loving wife and happy family, surrounded with everything necessary to make life enjoyable; and then flashed upon the scene that same family, after the demon of drink had cursed the home and brought want and desolation to the household, wan cheeks to the trusting wife, scant clothing to the children, with no chance to attend school, while Hope, the last solace of the poor and wretched, had fled forever from that home. There is one criticism upon his writings, both prose and poem. He was so full of words that they almost sparked in and through his compositions, and many would say there was an unnecessary number of words to express the ideas. This is probably true, but he not only designed expressing ideas, but also intended to clothe those ideas in language which would attract, and even charm. And after the criticism has been made, and we have again gone over his writings, we feel like there is such a fitness in the words used, and so much of the dove-tailed exactness of words into ideas, that we feel like saying, the beauty and charm would be marred if we were to subtract anything from it. It is like the scene of a wonderfully starry night, when the heavens are filled with the beauty of the coruscations,²¹ as compared with the same heavens, only bedecked with few stars.

Buck Owen was also a lawyer of no mean attainments. He was a young man in the practice at the beginning of the civil war, yet he had been retained in many important civil cases and in most of the criminal cases in his county of a grave character, and his reputation as a criminal lawyer had extended throughout the district in which he lived. When the secession movement came about, Buck Owen opposed it; but after his state cast her lot with the Confederacy he no longer held out. He enlisted in the 10th Mississippi Volunteers as a private soldier, and served as such for some time, when he was elected a first lieutenant. Only recently I was talking with an old soldier who served with him as a private soldier, and he spoke in the highest terms of his suave and gentle manners, and what a fine companionable man he was, and how attentive he was to the rights and interests of others, and what a store of information he possessed and how willing he was to talk to and for the benefit of a common soldier. On the last day of December, 1862, while leading his company in a gallant charge in the bloody battle of Murfreesboro, Tennessee, Buck Owen surrendered his life in the cause of his country. The pen could no more give us the rhythm of beauty and the orator never again entrance his audience with his oratory. Can it be true that "'tis all of life to live and all of death to die?" Surely there is some home beyond, where the immortal powers shall expand and bloom forever. Shall not Buck Owen again, in the far away ages to come, look into the face of that first born babe, whose love and innocence he celebrated in that beautiful poem, and clasp her to his fatherly heart forever?

March 9, 1906

Really Eli Phillips was all things to all men; that is, he adapted himself to all society and antagonized but few. In 1858 he ran for Probate clerk in old Itawamba county. It was thought still to be very politic not to be offering for office against the "Simon Pures" as such. But Colonel Moore, who was the Probate clerk, had had the office so long that he began to think he had a fee simple title to it. Eli Phillips had affiliated with Know Nothings the last general election, and many even of his strong friends did not believe he could be elected. But Richmond was a strong hold of the old Whig and Know Nothing parties, and there were several candidates offering, and Eli had the sagacity and good judgement to say nothing about parties, unless compelled to do so, and then to make the point that the office for which he was running was not a political office at all, and should be given to a good man irrespective of his politics. Moore did not consider Phillips a dangerous opponent and most directed his attention to others whom he considered more formidable, which Phillips made the point, that still moves on down the ages, that Moore had been in office long enough, and some new man should be allowed to learn something of the office. Again, Phillips had the shrewdness to concentrate all his leading party men on himself, with special instructions not to show their hands. Besides, Eli Phillips was very popular at his home box, and it was only second in size in the county, and so when the votes were counted out he got almost every vote at Richmond and a small scattering vote throughout the county, and came in by a small plurality, and when the vote was counted and the result determined, Colonel Moore, the clerk of long standing, said, "There's been a wonderful[12] land slide in two years."

Eli Phillips was one man who electioneered from the time he was first elected until he went out of office which was about thirteen years, and he was the only man I ever knew who knew when to quit running for one office and then what office to offer for next so as to be successful. When he was first elected it was by a mere plurality, and the most of those votes, as I have heretofore said, came from his home box Richmond, but he had a few staunch friends at every box in the county. He had, however, many strong men who opposed him very bitterly. How to win them for the next contest was the problem which confronted him. If it were possible, he treated those men better even than his best and warmest admirers, and by the time the next election came on, practically he had no opposition. No man ever asked for a favor which was within his power that he failed to grant. I now recall an incident in which he showed his diplomacy to advantage. In those olden times before the war if a probate clerk, whose duty it then was under the law to issue marriage license, should he issue a license without the authority of the parent or guardian where the child was under twenty-one if a male

84

or eighteen if a female, he subjected himself to suit for one thousand dollars by the parent or guardian of such minor. Even where a clerk was ever so careful he sometimes made a mistake and got into trouble. Thus it happened with Phillips in issuing a license for the marriage of old Major Black's daughter. The Major was a high strung South Carolinian by birth and raising, coming to this county in the late forties or early fifties. He was and always had been a great friend to Eli, and was himself very much disturbed on account of coming in conflict with him in this way, but he told Phillips although he was a good friend and admirer of his he would be bound to sue him for the thousand dollar penalty for such cases provided. Eli said, "alright Major, but one thing I wish above all things and that is that this lawsuit shall not interfere with our friendship. That is dearer to me than money." To this the Major agreed, but told Phillips he might look out for the suit right away as he had retained Russ Beene to file suit and it would be forth coming. Phillips was well aware of Major Black's weakness for anything and everything in the favor of South Carolina, and so he had his little son Sumter to memorise a patriotic piece of poetry in relation to the war, which was just then coming on, in which South Carolina was given the pre-eminence in her stand for the Southland. The next time the Major came to town Phillips again reminded him of the fact that their friendship must not be broken on account of the lawsuit, but never for one moment intimated that he did not want the suit brought. Eli said, "now, Major, to show you that we are still friends and that we propose to remain so, come on and take dinner with me as you have been doing when in town." So the Major went to dinner with Eli and he was treated as he had been before, and after dinner was over the little son, who was quite sprightly, and clever, was dressed up in a becoming manner for the occasion, having a small South Carolina flag, and Phillips had him to get up and speak the poetry, lauding South Carolina and her action in seceding from the Union, to the skies. When he had finished, Major Black seemed wonderfully pleased, and after waiting awhile he requested that the boy repeat the speech. When he had repeated it, Black slapped his hand and stamped his feet, and said "Phillips,

I'll swear that's a clever boy." After some time spent at the residence of Phillips, they returned to the court house and the Major repeated several times that he hated to bring a suit against an old friend and a Carolinian, as Eli was. But, Eli said, "That makes no difference, Major, you will never find me falling out with a friend, and especially you, for doing what he conceives to be his duty." When Black got ready to start home that evening he told Phillips to tell Beene to hold up on the suit until he heard further from him.

As he went on that evening toward home, with his thought on old South Carolina and the little son speaking so eloquently of her glory and renown, it was too much for him, and he stopped on the way and wrote a note to Colonel Beene and ordered the suit stopped at once, and he and Phillips were the best of friends so long as the Major lived.

BUSINESSMEN
February 9, 1906

This history would not be complete if I were to wind up these Pen Pictures so soon as I had given a sketch of the lawyers who were practicing at Fulton when I went there in the heyday of my young manhood. While my association was closer with most of the lawyers than any others, still I was not at all indifferent to the actions, movements and merits of citizens following other professions and employments.

M. C. Cummings was connected with the history and life of Fulton for a longer period of time than any other man whom I ever knew. He did not live in the town, but about one mile north in the country for all the time I knew him, but he was so closely interwoven with the woof and warp of the town that everybody considered Uncle Mack a resident. Besides, he lived there in the earlier years before I knew him. Many, many years ago he came to Fulton a poor boy, having nothing, and worked for those who were in better circumstances, chopping wood at their wood piles, as I have been informed, at fifty cents a day. He was a man of limited education, not really being able to speak the King's English with any accuracy, and I do not suppose he ever studied English Grammar a day in his life. But he was a man of fine judgement in his business, that of farming, milling, stock raising and trading. He had as fine capacity as any man I ever knew of turning everything he touched into gold. The four bits which he made working by the day, he carefully kept for a rainy day, as the expression goes, and then, when the rainy day came, he still added to it until he had enough to begin making investments. He made very few mistakes in his investments. Soon after he came to Fulton it was generally thought he had tuberculosis, and many predicted an early death from that dread disease; but he lived so much out doors, and such an active life, and was so full of energy, that he lived to about eighty-five. He was simple in his diet, and never drank anything to intoxicate, worked much and planned more. From the time I knew Mr. Cummings to the day of his death, I never knew him to be without the means of accommodating those who wished to pay for it. If you wanted a horse, or a horse and buggy, all you had to do was to call on Uncle Mack, and during slavetime, if you wanted a cook for a week, or a month, or a negro man for a day's work, all you had to do was to ask him, and you were accommodated. He had fine discrimination in making trades, and was a good judge of men as well. When the war came on he was in good shape financially, his property then being worth at least a hundred thousand dollars. Many men before the war invested all they had in negro property, save the small amount it took to buy a country home for the negroes to work on; but Cummings was too wise a man and far seeing financier to do that. When the war came up, in addition to his lands and mill, he laid up a reasonable stock of gold, and owed nothing; so that when the negroes were freed, he was still a man of some means, and still possessed that indomitable will and wonderful energy which had carried him through so many struggles. He went to work after losing his negro property as if nothing had happened of an adverse nature. Soon after the war when cotton was high, but growing higher, a fortuitous circumstance came to him, and he had the good judgement and sagacity to embrace it. One evening two gentlemen, riding fine horses, rode up to his gate and asked to remain over night. This was readily accorded them, as this was always one of the money making means of Mr. Cummings. It was at a time when feed for horses was scarce, and each of the horsemen had a long small sack of oats, which they told Cummings they carried to feed on at such places as they could not get feed. Mr. Cummings thought this rather a strange tale, for two reasons; first, the sacks would only hold enough feed for about two days, and in the second place, they were careful to carry their oat sacks up stairs to the rooms assigned them. After supper these gentlemen called Uncle Mack up to their room and told him that they had been told that he was altogether responsible and reliable, and a man to whom they might confide everything they had and it was true they had oats in their sacks, the oats were only there to hide the gold they were carrying. They also told Mr. Cummings that they had been told that he was well acquainted with every hog path and by way in the county, knew the people perfectly, had a fine influence with them, and could buy more cotton than any man in the county, and they were anxious to employ him to buy cotton for them, and offered him a fine price for his work and his influence. At once the possibilities of the opportunity flashed into the mind of Uncle Mack, and his far seeing discretion told him that he was to be hewer of wood nor drawer of water for these northern fellows, but that he himself must be an independent dealer. They put it to him in every conceivable way, keeping him up till midnight endeavoring him to accept. But no, he had business of his own requiring his special attention. Finally they gave it up for the night, but hoping to succeed better in the morning. But they did not know the man with whom they were dealing. Cummings had resurrected his little stock of gold from beneath the old pine trees where it had rested all through the war, and, although the strangers kept him up so late, he was on the road and far out in the country before daylight, with sufficiency of gold for one day's work. His plan was to buy all the cotton he could and pay as little cash for it as possible, giving his note for the balance to be paid when the cotton should be removed, and giving papers to that effect. Often he could buy cotton for five dollars cash on the bale, as everyone knew him to be entirely responsible. Cummings kept his own counsel, and left his wife to take care of the gentlemen when they came down to breakfast. When the strangers came down to breakfast, which they did a little late, as they had been up late the night before, they failed to find Mr. Cummings, and could get no trace of his whereabouts. In the meantime, he was "making hay while the sun shone." He traversed the country from one side to the other, and wherever people would sell cotton he bought, until he had all the cotton in the country, with only a small payment made generally, and his note given for the balance to be paid before the cotton should be moved. Wherever the strangers went to buy, they found Cummings had preceded them, and secured all the cotton to be had. Finally they began making overtures to Cummings to buy his cotton, and he made a trade with them by which he made net off the cotton he had bought over twenty thousand dollars in gold. Few men would have been able to have seen the possibilities that lay in the road to success in this matter. Uncle Mack was always an independent dealer, never working for wages after he saved up enough to transact business on his own account. He always thought that the advance in price in the market of any article you might buy was a better business than working for another on salary; and then besides, he loved the thought of independent action.

September 15, 1905

I feel that while I am speaking of men and things of the olden time, I cannot have a subject more interesting than Colonel R. C. Clark, who lived for many years at Verona, and died there some ten years ago. I knew but very little of Colonel Clark before the war, he only having moved to Verona about 1860. But he was a very interesting character, and from whose life we may draw some valuable lessons. Unless there are some things to be said of a man's life which may be helpful to others, or unless there are interesting incidents connected with the life, or unless some warning can be given from his failings, time is wasted in publishing even a short synopsis of anyone's life; but if we can hold up the history of anyone as worthy of following, or where pleasurable incidents can be rehearsed, which are not hurtful, or where we can hold up the subject as one erring and thereby indicate how we may avoid the same, or like errors, the writing may be well published.

Colonel Clark was born near Petersburg, Virginia early in the nineteenth century. His father died when he was about eleven years old, and he then went to Mobile, Alabama and lived with an uncle until he was about seventeen years old, when he returned to live with and assist his mother. His father was a thriftless kind of man, and not only did he not accumulate anything for the family, but he left them as a heritage a debt of about five or six thousand dollars fixed on the home. In the course of a few years his widow, the mother of Colonel Clark, paid off the debt by strict economy and good management, and then with that discernment characteristic of a good financier, she decided that the course of empire in the United States was westward; and so she determined to invest in Alabama and remove there herself. In this determination young Richard agreed, showing thus early those far-seeing qualities in business and finance which enabled him to afterward accomplish so much in the financial world.

While staying with his uncle in Mobile, he was faithfully and well trained in business and business principles, and was often entrusted by his uncle with important matters, which were always performed with fidelity and ability for one so young. He was often compelled in the discharge of his duties in business for his uncle to go from Mobile to Columbus, Mississippi. The trips were made on horseback, carrying an extra horse as a pack horse, and being attended by an Indian. There was no such good luck as putting up with some settler on the way, but they had to camp out in the wild woods among the wild beasts of the forest. On one of the trips, Colonel Clark killed a deer, and cutting off the ham, placed it on his pack horse for use on the way out. That night he and his Indian camped out as usual, and soon after dark, the wolves in great numbers came trooping in, attracted by the flavor of the venison, howling as they came, and nearer and still nearer they came in increasing numbers and with louder and fiercer howls, until both the colonel and his Indian thought prudence the better part of valor, and so each climbed up a tree, carrying, however, their pistols with them, which they fired off towards the varmints every once and awhile through the night, for the protection of their animals. Every time they fired their pistols, the wolves would scamper off, only, however, to return again; and this kept up till about daylight next morning, when they retired entirely, permitting the Colonel and his Indian friend to come down from their nightly perch in the trees, make their breakfast and pursue their journey, to their great delight. Neither slept any that night. I have heard the expression all my life, that it looks so and so "to a man up a tree," but I guess young Richard and his Indian friend had a more vivid experience as to how things looked up a tree that night than any of my readers have ever had or are likely to have.

Colonel Clark only went to school a few months in his whole life. But that does not mean that he had no education. On the contrary, after he had a family, and after he had been chosen a trustee of Lagrane college, Alabama, he studied and recited of nights, after his day's work was over, and by this means learned much; and then his uncommon sound sense and good judgement enabled him to separate the chaff from the wheat in his extensive reading and large observation. Colonel Clark was a farmer for many years, but all the while a born trader, and his discomment[23] of the right thing to buy and the right time to buy it, enabled him to succeed financially. When the war came up he had accumulated a considerable estate, which was largely dissipated by the result of the war. Beginning almost at the bottom again, as he had done at the first, he took charge of the different mercantile firms at Verona and Tupelo, and by his careful and prudent management, they all succeeded well, and brought success and profit to him and all who were connected with him. Few men were better judges of men and business transactions than Colonel Clark.

I remember an instance in which his wise counsel proved the financial salvation of a friend. That friend owed Colonel Clark's firms about fifteen to twenty thousand dollars, and all his lands were mortgaged for its payments, and the gentleman having had several bad crops, was much discouraged and ready to turn every thing over to Colonel for payment. But Colonel Clark assured him that by a few good crops and management he could pay out, and that his lands would in a few years be worth many times the money he owed. And thus by taking the Colonel's advice, he paid out, and I suppose those lands are now worth one hundred thousand dollars. Many men situated as Colonel Clark then was would not only have taken the land, but would have forced the sale to get them; for I know that with Colonel Clark's discernment and sagacity, he could see the value of those lands in the then near future, so his advice must have been disinterested. His rule through life was to take no man's home on whom he had a mortgage only as a last resort. Let us imitate his virtues and learn lessons of wisdom from his life of success.

PREACHERS
March 23, 1906

Heretofore in these "Pen Pictures," I have said nothing about the ministry, but I would not have my readers suppose we had no preachers in those olden times, nor that I was then or am now indifferent to them or their preaching. When we came to Mississippi, or even up to 1855, there were no pastorates in old Itawamba county, even in the best towns. When we came in 1840 I do not think there was a church house in the county unless it was at Fulton, and I do not think they had a church building there. The Indians only left here in 1836 and 1837, and after they left, and the white people came in they had first to build some kind of houses to live in and then get enough people together to make at least a small congregation before they could build church houses. Previous to this the people assembled for worship at school houses or at the residence of some settler. I know my father used to have preaching at his house in those early days. The Methodists have always pursued the policy of having preachers on the ground as soon as the cabins were built or tents erected. The general rule with ministers, though, in those early days was the preacher worked in his farm or blacksmith shop, or stood behind the counter during the week and preached every sabbath, receiving therefore but little if any pay.

The Methodists had many local preachers who filled the pulpits of the Methodist churches on days not occupied by the regular circuit riders, even of charges where there were regular ministers filling their appointments for they had preaching only once a month by the regular ministers in all this country in those days.

The first preacher I remember seeing at my father's house was Lock E. Hankins, afterward circuit clerk of Itawamba county. He was then on the circuit. I remember but little of his preaching that early, as I was so young, but I heard him later, and know that he was a very earnest preacher, but as old Uncle Burt Moore put it, "a little scattering." There was a very considerable difference between the preaching then and now. There is doubtless more learning and research thrown into a sermon now than then; but the old-time sermon was not wanting in zeal, enthusiasm and spirituality. Men have been trained in a different line of thought of late years, and their opportunities for educational advantages have increased very materially. But it would be a rather difficult problem to undertake to make an old-timer believe that the preaching of the present day is more helpful to the hearers than that which we heard in the long ago.

There was a Methodist minister in the old days of Itawamba who was a very popular preacher, named Alex S. Hamilton, and who was really a preacher of power. He was rather eccentric, and very excitable. When the war came he raised a company, went into service, was elected Lieutenant Colonel of the 1st Mississippi Regiment of Infantry. He would fight all the week and preach on Sunday, unless it should be a fighting Sunday. Many men situated as he was, being exempt from military service, would never have heard a cannon boom, nor come in sight of an enemy. But he, laying aside all legal rights of exemption from military service, and having in view the good of his country, forgot, as it were, for the time being, his sacred calling, and heard only the call of his country for help. The truth is Colonel Hamilton was a military man, had a martial name, came of a fighting South Carolina stock, and if he had been compelled to remain at home while the fight was going on around him he would have been as a caged lion. He would have chafed and worn his life away against the bars of fate which thus confined him. It may be he was not as true to his Lord as his sacred calling required, but when he saw the waving plume of the battle flag and heard the cry of his bleeding country for help, and saw the scarcity of true and brave men, I feel like the compassionate Lord will make many allowances for his want of full devotion to his sacred calling by reason of his great devotion to and sacrifice for the love of country. I hope he may not rest the heavier beneath the clod for want of strictly following his higher calling and being led into the service of his country.

April 6, 1906

The ministers of the long ago still linger on my hands, but I hope my readers will not become weary of reading of them. You know, "like priests, like people" is a saying of the olden time. There is much truth in the saying. If the preachers of the country are God fearing men, leading the people right by their pious and Godly example, the people are apt to follow in a large measure in the same course; while on the other hand, if the ministers are looking out alone for self, and profess to be following in the way of righteousness because of the "loaves and fishes" which they get, God save the people! I have now to speak of some more ministers of old Itawamba who lived among us in the long ago, and who made their living largely by their own labor on the farm or whose living was obtained by the work of their slaves.

In the long ago I only remember one preacher of the Christian denomination and that was old Uncle Nat King, who lived about ten miles south of old Fulton, but used to preach at Fulton. He was a tall man, about six feet two inches, large bald head, full of sense, but possessing but a limited education. Uncle Nat had been a fighter in his time, not willing but when forced on him he was known to whip three men all on him at once in the old old time, before the war, at Fulton. But naturally he was a man of peace. I used to hear him preach at Fulton. A Dr. Davis was one of his faith, and was generally present when Brother King preached. He was a strong man, notwithstanding his want of education. He had read and thought much of the Book of Books. I have heard him preaching at the top of his voice often and then stop and come down to an ordinary tone with "aint that so Brother Dock?" Again, if he thought he had preached long enough, right in the midst of his discourse he would stop and say, "Brother Dock, have I preached long enough?" and if Brother Dock said yes, he would raise his large sunburned hand and say "let us receive the benediction."

Another old time preacher, whom I knew in those early times, was Mr. John Burdine, who lived near Andrews Chapel in old Itawamba county. I do not think I ever heard John Burdine preach, but have heard him conclude sermons for others, which we used to call exhorting. He was rather a frail man from the time I first knew him, and did but little preaching after. He was in comfortable circumstances financially, and did not rely upon his preaching for a living. He was rather a heavy made man, sallow complexioned, clean shaved, heavy eyebrows and a keen and piercing eye. He was a Methodist of the old school, so to speak, by which I mean he was intensely Methodist. He was a man of strong opinions and strong feelings, making up his judgement on any proposition and never changing. I remember at the time I came to the bar, there was a law suit pending in the circuit court at Fulton, which had been appealed, from a Justice court, in which Dave Traylor was plaintiff and John Burdine was defendant, and in which at the final wind up, Traylor only claimed that he was entitled to have judgement for two cents, in order that he might not have to pay the costs, which amounted to about one thousand dollars. But Burdine was successful, and would have carried the case to supreme court, if he could have done so before he would have paid it. He felt sure he was in the right, and the rule he made was to make no compromise when in the right. I am writing history and not commending this trait in his character, but those who knew John Burdine never questioned his uprightness.

November 24, 1905

A. B. Bullard was a lawyer in full practice when I went to Fulton in 1859. He was also a minister of the gospel, and a very eloquent preacher. He was rather an ungainly man in his personal appearance, being about six feet tall, somewhat stooped, large feet, legs bowed, large prominent teeth, high forehead, deep set, or rather sunken eyes, coal black, with scattering dark hair and large, prominent nose. His eyes were very bright and expressive, and when under his enthusiasm and pressure of some public discussion, his eyes flashed fire, as the saying goes.

I remember hearing him preach a sermon in about 1858 at old Bethlehem five miles east of Tupelo which I have always considered a model of pulpit eloquence. The chapter he read, that wonderful fifth chapter of Daniel, clings to my mind through all the changing scenes of life as though it were but last week. And after he had announced his text, "Tekel," and began painting the scenes of that lordly banquet, in the magnificent palace of Babylon, where were assembled the glory and chivalry of the empire, with his eyes flashing fire, and every movement of his body in unison with the subject, the audience were carried away by the power of his eloquence, and almost raised up in their seats, their interest was so great. And finally, when he came to the point in the scene where Belshazzar stood with one of the golden vessels in his hand, taken from the Temple at Jerusalem, and raised the same to drink the wine therefrom, the speaker glanced toward the top of the house and said,

At this point fingers of an unseen hand appeared and wrote against the golden candle stick taken from God's house on the plaster of the King's palace strange characters and fashioned them into strange words, fiery character and burning which portended evil to the King and his lords, and which none of them could read. Terror took hold on the King, his countenance became ashen hue, the joints of his loins were loosened, his knees smote one against another, and wreck and ruin seemed to lie hanging over his head, and hope no longer beckoned him to something better. He fairly screamed for the soothsayers, astrologers and wise men to come and read and interpret the hand writing on the wall.

And the action of the speaker as he described the fingers of the man's hand by which he held up his own long right arm and grasped an invisible pen with his large bony fingers, and moved them as the fingers of the unknown at Babylon as they wrote, was electrical. And when he came to describe the condition of the lost sinner, weighed in the balances and found wanting, weighed in his own balances, and in God's balances, wanting toward himself, his neighbor and his God; wanting toward his country and wanting toward society; wanting in time and wanting to all eternity, then he lifted aside the veil and gave us a word picture of the lost ones, forever lost, on account of want of weight, weighed and found wanting, because Christ the meek and lowly one of Gallilee, had never come into their lives and sanctified their hearts.

Turning with enthusiasm and brightness from this subject to the world's hope and the christian's solace, he cheered the believer in the promise of the Savior's heavenly home and the life beyond this vale of sorrows.

I have in my mind's eye another sermon which I heard him preach from the judge's stand at the court house at Fulton in September 1860. The occasion was that of the funeral of Burge Gaither, who died at Fulton early in September 1860, just after the September term of the Circuit Court was over. Burge Gaither was a strong Methodist, and Bullard was a minister in the Cumberland Presbyterian church but they were such staunch friends that Gaither made request that Bullard should preach his funeral. Burge Gaither was an old time ante bellum gentleman, having as many friends as anyone who ever lived in Fulton and at the time of his death was a candidate for county treasurer, and it was almost universally conceded that his election was assured. He had a wife and three children surviving him, and one dying only a few days before he did, a poor man, whose residence had been burned about a year before he was called away, and to us it seemed as important and necessary for Burge Gaither to live for the comfort and even support of his family as any man who had ever lived. When the day came for the funeral, the court house was crowded to overflowing, his friends from many parts of the county coming to pay their last respects, and all Fulton was out en masse, all anxious also to hear the eloquent tribute of the gifted preacher. I recall now as if yesterday the solemn and interesting scene, the packed house, the solemn calm, the upturned faces and watery eyes and heaving bosoms; the widow's weeds and the three clinging little orphans, the ascent to the judge's stand as a pulpit for the preacher, whose high and lofty forehead and bright sparkling eyes showed unusual intelligence, and whose manner clearly indicated that he realized both the importance and solemnity of the occasion. Before him sat the beauty and chivalry of the county, but there also sat the widow and orphans of the preacher's dead friend, and therefore what to say and how to say it was the problem of the divine. I can say as I now remember it he met and mastered the issue well and nobly. God's ways are not man's ways, because God's power and God's wisdom are so much greater than man's, even as the heavens are higher than the earth. The preacher spoke of the mighty and wonderful size of the Alps and the Andes, the Rockies and Himalayas, and yet God weighed them in his balances; he pictured to us the extent of the seas and the oceans and the wonderful overflowing volumes of the rivers, and still God measures them all in the hollow of His hand; he scanned the far distant stars and the system of stars, so far from us that if some of them should be blotted out today they would still shine on for a million years, and no grain of them all not in His mind and every particle numbered. And the same God who possessed such wonderful power, had also all wisdom and infinite love, and the widow and the orphans of his dead friend would be the special care and under the guidance of this Divine One. We cannot understand, but He knows the end from the beginning and all the way between. The sermon was a masterpiece of eloquence, and fully sustained the reputation of the speaker.

December 1, 1905

I have heard my preacher brother say that Bullard told him that he promised his God when he began the practice of the law that if he were prospered for fifteen years he would return to the ministry again and devote his whole time to preaching the gospel. He was very successful financially, having accumulated some thirty thousand dollars and I think the fifteen year limit was drawing to a close when the war closed. But he made one mistake in his invest-ments, having bought negro property altogether, and even sold his country home and plantation in 1864 and received pay therefor in negro property altogether. So, when the war closed, he lost all, not even owning a residence.

He was a very fine lawyer and an excellent practitioner. He was logical, eloquent and well grounded in legal principles, good on reply and strong on summing up a cause. In going to and from the courts in the adjoining counties, he rode a very large sorrel mule, instead of riding or driving a fine horse, as most men would have done in his circumstances. I remember going with him to the Sep-tember term of the Circuit Court of Pontotoc county in 1860. On our return I left him before we reached Tupelo, which was then in its infancy. I guess Bullard's sorrel mule had never seen a locomo-tive or train of cars, nor heard a whistle. The railroad was just beginning to run trains through the Old Reliable at the time I speak of, and Bullard afterwards told me of this incident in relation to himself and the mule as he returned. As he got on the track of the railroad at the crossing, an engine whistled above, and the mule become affrighted and turned right down the track south, making the best headway possible, and he was wholly unable to turn the mule to the right or to the left. After the animal had gone some distance down the road, an incoming train whistled from below with that wild danger scream calculated to frighten stock, when Bullard's mule, not able to stand between two fires, jumped the track and took to the woods, and he was not able to check her speed till she entered old Town Creek bottom. In thinking of this incident I have often thought no wonder the mule acted so strangely. If we had never at any time heard of a railroad and train of cars and locomotive, nor heard their scream, nor seen their wonderful head-light, flashing out like a fire furnace seven times heated, and all on a sudden, some dark night, as we should be passing through some lone wood, the rumbling wells of the oncoming of the train should be heard in the near distance, while the stars were keeping their sentinels above, showing it could be no cyclone, and at the proper distance, we should see and hear for the first time the headlight and the thousand times worse than panther scream, how much better would we act than the poor mule? We would be like the poor ignorant people in 1832 when the "stars fell."[24] This I do not remember, not having been then born, but have heard my father and mother speak of it often. They were neither philosophers nor astronomers, nor had they ever read of meteoric showers, and they did not know what was coming, but father was an upright man fearing not what God might bring, and mother was not only a christian, but a woman of wonderful courage under all difficulties, and so they weathered the storm all right. But a tenant on father's place thought surely the judgment day had come, and was praying for help, and finally he said to my father, "Collier, the world's certainly coming to an end. Look yonder how few stars are in the heavens." My father said he looked towards the east and saw the day dawn was coming, and of course the stars were dimming under the advance of the sun. Pardon this digression from Bullard and his mule and the screaming locomotive.

NOTES

[1] Probably A. H. Moore whose home was on the Mantachie River in Itawamba County.
[2] John Mitchener.
[3] Tombigbee River.
[4] Other records cite 7 miles.
[5] Originally from Thomas A. Kempis' 14th Century *Imitation of Christ*, but appropriated by Benjamin Franklin and others.
[6] A. B. Bullard, also a minister.
[7] J. L. Finley.
[8] O. H. Whitfield.
[9] Lawyer and singer of Fulton.
[10] Lawyer, politician, poet of Fulton.
[11] Henry Moore.
[12] S. J. Gholson, federal judge before the Civil War.
[13] Davis was also commander of the state's forces during the Civil War and later author of *Recollections of Mississippi and Mississippians*, which mentions Clayton and which Clayton greatly admired.
[14] Clayton corrects Quincy to Athens in a May 4, 1906, "Pen Picture."
[15] A. J. McWilliams.
[16] Clayton often refers to Mooreville as "Mooresville," perhaps indicating a shift from the possessive "Moore's ville."
[17] A political party opposing reduction in the amount of paper money in circulation.

[18] Also spelled "Bogue Phalia" and "Bogue Foliah."

[19] A secret political organization hostile to the political influence of recent immigrants and Roman Catholics.

[20] Two miles south of Nettleton in Monroe County.

[21] Sparkling stars.

[22] Strange.

[23] Knowledge.

[24] Actually, this landmark event in Alabama history occurred the night of November 12-13, 1833, when, as one witness said, "thousands of luminous meteors were shooting across the firmament in every direction."

CHAPTER IV

Requiem For A Lost Cause

A YOUNG MAN AT WAR
1861–1865

*No man knows just how he will feel and act in a battle till
he has tried it. I only know one thing in relation to it,
and that is I would not RUN.*

*Those familiar with more graphic descriptions of the disastrous
effects of war will find Clayton's reminiscences of the Civil War
remarkably bloodless in comparison. While Clayton does not hide his
dismay at the destruction and loss of life which accompanies armed
conflict, his personal vision of the war is one of romantic melancholy
for a heroic venture which signaled the violent passing of a way of
life. Men do not die; they "fall." Bullets "sing" and shells "whistle."
There is no talk of death around the campfire; instead, soldiers sing,
"piddle," and light-heartedly chase rabbits and squirrels. Confron-
tations with the enemy are exciting adventures in which Southern
heroes perform deeds of valor with little thought to the consequences, only that one's "honor" on the battlefield must be preserved.*

*Certainly, though, his descriptions are filled with the insight and
detail of a soldier who served with the Confederate cavalry from
1861 until a few weeks after the surrender of Lee at Appomattox in*

1865. Commissioned as a captain, Clayton fought with Southern armies in west Tennessee and northeast Mississippi, and participated in the final defense of Atlanta before following Sherman's troops in their infamous march to the sea. Although Clayton's vision of the war is romantic, these sketches are solidly grounded in fact. Names, dates, and troop movements presented in the "Pen Pictures" match almost invariably with historical information.

Though Clayton romanticizes the war, it is obvious from his emphasis on the devastation of the South and its people that he is serious in his plea that the "nation never put on the war paint again." As he nears the end of these war reminiscences, he describes a burning railroad depot which is obviously symbolic of the lost cause and of the heroic ideal that has been lost with it. As Clayton depicts a stranger standing among the wreckage, he seems to be rendering a final desolate portrait of the destructiveness of war and of the ruin of his beloved South:

> When we returned to the depot place, where ruin and desolation reigned, and saw the ascending smoke of the recent fires of the enemy, the lone stranger still stood like a wandering Arab looking on the wreck of his home land.

June 1, 1906

If you had had your eyes fixed on the road from Fulton to Pontotoc on the second Monday of September, 1860, you might have seen two horsemen wending their way from the former to the latter named town. One of the men was a man of say fifty, the other was a young man of twenty-four,[1] both lawyers, attending the Circuit Court at Pontotoc, the older one looking after business, the younger one seeking to extend his acquaintanceship with the bar of the District, and hoping that some poor man in trouble might call on him for help. The day was of that mellow, balmy, sunshiny kind which the South only can furnish, with the faintest breath of coming fall, the fields flecked with the fleecy staple, the red berries of the sumach flashing by the roadside, and the variegated colors of the rainbow interwoven in every valley and hillside, wherever the forests still stood intact. And when the sun sank beneath the western hills, throwing back ten thousand coruscations of glory, it presented a scene to be remembered for a lifetime. When these lawyers had saluted the judge and mingled with their brethren of the bar to their satisfaction, they returned toward old Fulton together. But before they had passed the half way station, the young man excused himself for failing to accompany his friend any further, and deflected to the left of the main road in order to see a good woman who owed him a fee for professional services rendered, which in his then impecunious condition, would have added much to the weight of his pocketbook. When the young man approached the country home, it being late in the afternoon, and remembering what plenty they had in store, he thought to remain overnight; and this purpose was fixed to a full determination when he approached the entrance and there saw a beautiful and lovely maiden, just entering the threshold of womanhood, and whose cheeks were suffused with telltale blushes as she bade him welcome. And so it was, that the young man could say in the language of Caesar, "Veni, vide, vici, I came, I saw, I conquered," and, instead of asking the good matron for the little money which she owed him, he plead for and received the promise of her daughter in marriage ere he closed his eyes in sleep that beautiful September night. This was not far from the middle of September, and that young man went no more to see the hope and light of his life till the 27th day of November, of the same year, when he went to bring her home, and only wrote and received one letter in the mean time. What think you of this young men and fair maidens, who visit and receive the promised one three times a week and remain and are detained till after midnight each visit?

But, friends and fellow countrymen, when the hymeneal kiss had been given, and the young husband had carried his fair young bride to his own home, the far distant lightning could be seen and the far off rumbling of the thunder could be heard in the political firmament, portending the wonderful hurricane which soon spread over the Southland and blackened her fair fields and lovely vales. Every man who took the platform to deliver an address, painted in glowing colors the heroism and constance of our forefathers of

Revolutionary fame in winning for us our liberty, and then urged everyone to be worthy sons of such magnificent sires. And then the poet joined in with:

> Breathes the man with the soul so dead,
> Who never to himself hath said,
> This is my own, my native land!
> Whose heart hath ne'er within him burned,
> As home his footsteps he hath turned,
> From wandering on a foreign strand!
> If such there breathe, go, mark him well;
> For him no minstrel raptures swell;
> High though his titles, proud his name,
> Boundless his wealth as wish can claim;
> Despite those titles, power and pelf,
> The wretch, concentrated all in self,
> Living, shall forfeit fair renown,
> And, doubly dying, shall go down
> To the vile dust from whence he sprung,
> Unwept, unhonored, and unsung.[2]

The young husband looked at his fair and lovely bride and thought of his obligations to her, and then considered his duty to his country, and was undecided. Then came to his mind the magnificent outburst of patriotism contained in the Southern poet's "Land of the South," in which he painted in vivid colors the "imperial" Southland, its sweet scenes sit, fair skies, its on-rolling rivers, its hills and valleys blooming with health and green with verdure, even surpassing the wonderful land of Italy; and then threw upon the canvas freedom's pinions, waving in peace, while science cast her pearls around and religion lifted her sacred dome above, and the fair maidens bloomed like sylvan flowers, having hearts as pure as crystal, and in the closing verse, burst forth in these patriotic strains:

> Land of the South! imperial land!
> Then here's a health to thee
> Long as thy mountain barrier stand,
> May'st thou be blest and free!

> May dark dissension's banner ne'er
> Wave o'er thy fertile loam,
> But should it come, there's one will die
> To save his native home![3]

And that *one*, touched the heart of the young husband, and decided his mind for his native land rather than to stay at home with
his young wife; and that *one*, spread like wildfire throughout old
Itawamba, and went into every nook and corner of Mississippi,
bringing forth magnificent soldiers; that *one*, came leaping down
from the "Dark and Bloody Ground" of old Kentucky, with its
legions ready for the conflict; that *one*, spread from the vine-clad
hills and beautiful valleys of Tennessee toward the center of the
Confederacy, like a snow ball, gathering strength and power as it
came; that *one*, swam the mighty Mississippi from Missouri, with
General Price[4] and landed his hosts for home and native land; that
one, took the Arkansas Tooth-Picks from the Savannas of that wonderful land and distributed them from Texas to Virginia; that *one*,
kissed the outstretching prairies of the Lone Star State of Texas and
they bloomed like the rose of Sharon, and multiplied like their own
wild flowers bringing forth Rangers and Cowboys for the defense
of our homes and our firesides; that *one*, turned loose the Tigers and
Zenaves of Louisiana to prey upon the enemies of their country;[5]
that *one*, crossed the Alabama, not to rest there, but to take from
her hills and vales, coves and mountains, swamps and canebrakes,
the men of action and renown who held high the banner during the
war; that *one*, flew like a screaming eagle over Georgia from Re-
sacca to Savannah gathering up the stay and strength of our armies;
that *one*, reached for the orange and the magnolia of Florida, and
spread over all the land; that *one*, sniffed the breeze and heard the
moan of the pines, and the rustle of the rushes of the Carolinas, and
the moan of their pines and the rustle of their rushes were
transformed into "plaided warriors armed for strife," worthy to
stand with Pickett[6] at Gettysburg, and fall by his side in that memorable charge; and that *one*, gathered round Lee and Jackson[7] from
old Virginia, valley men and mountaineers, whose breasts were ever
toward the enemy and their hearts toward the homeland; and when

that *one*, and this *one*, and the other *ones*, had all concentered under their different leaders, the *one*, became a mighty host indeed, so mighty and powerful that now, after forty years, the pensioners from our bullets and other casualties incident to the war, drawing pay from the treasury of the government, are more numerous than the army we had in the field, besides the killed and those who died from wounds and sickness.

And so it was that while these hosts were assembling at their different places of rendezvous, the young husband, with an unmarried brother, stood at the threshold of his father's home to bid farewell to father and mother and his young wife, just four months to a day from the day he gave his promise at the altar, in order to enter the service of his country. I paint you the picture with my pen, not because of the prominence of the parties, nor of any great reputation the parties may have made, but when I have flashed the picture upon the canvas, and you have looked upon the scene, you shall have beheld the condition of the South in the long ago years of 1861 and 1862.

Now, when you multiply this scene by the number of homes in the land, you can have some faint conception of the sorrow and anguish that wrung the hearts, and filled the Southland in those perilous days. May the God of all love grant that no such scenes may ever again wring the hearts and fill the homes of our loved country.

June 15, 1906

No man knows just how he will feel and act in a battle till he has tried it. I only know one thing in relation to it, and that is I would not RUN. My sense of honor, and the love and honor I bore to my father and mother, enabled me to say, I will not run; but as to how I would feel and act I had but little conception. The horse learns as soon as the man, too, in what the danger consists. You may ride a horse into a fight where the cannon are booming and the small arms cracking, and he will move on undismayed until the whistle of the shells or the singing of the bullets can be heard, and then he knows the danger even before he is hit, as well as a man does, and will shy from the sound of the bullet, when he would pay no attention to the sound of the report.

I remember having been in a fight in Collierville, Tennessee in about August, 1863,[8] in which we attacked the fortification; and we were ordered at one stage of the fight to lie down, and I was myself lying by the side of Nathan Riley, an Orderly Sergeant, and while we were loading and shooting I heard a whip-crack noise by my side, and he said, "I'm shot!" The wound was only a flesh wound in the thigh, though, and it seemed to me, and I always believed, if he had been carried to a good hospital, or to some private house where proper attention could have been given to him, he might have recovered. But he was carried through the country something like fifty miles to his country home, and the neglect and the wound together was too much for him and it proved fatal. If Nathan Riley had been a general or even a colonel, pages would long since have been written about his valor and constancy to duty, and his virtues would have been commended to the skies. But I feel as keenly in the matter and as kindly toward him as if he had worn a wreath on his collar and remained in the rear on some eminence and commanded the battle. Nathan Riley was a big souled and warm hearted man, a dear lover of his country, and ready to peril his life in her cause. Ah, Nathan, when last we were together, it was in the midst of danger and death; but we shall meet again where no smoke or fire shall intervene. There's but a span of earth which now separates between us and that shall soon be removed and we shall then see even as we are also seen.

My old friend, Tom Brooks, used to rib me considerably about a little incident that occurred at Wyatt, Mississippi where we were in a fight with the enemy. We were on the retreat and had to fight at the river long enough to enable us to cross over. It was in the fall of the year, and the rain was coming down with a constant patter, and we were on the side of a red hill, lying down loading and shooting as fast as we could, obeying orders. Finally we were ordered to cease firing, but still to lie down. Tom Brooks says I looked at him, and he was lying kinder on his knees and hands, with his body elevated considerably, a good mark for an enemy's bullet, and that I said to him, "Tom, you don't know how to lie down. You're trying to protect your body from the mud. Here's the way to lie down," and suiting the action to the word, he says I stretched myself out on the ground as flat as a pancake, showing how he might save his bacon.

Speaking of this Wyatt fight reminds me of an incident that occurred in relation to the number of the enemy we killed there. As we were retreating we had no time to ascertain what damage we may have done our foe; but some months afterward our command was again in the same neighborhood, and one of our boys dropped out and went over the field where the fight occurred. When he came back to the command he told me he knew we killed ONE man for there was a new made grave on the field where we had the fight. Nothing more was thought of the matter till about a year afterward, as we were riding one day in the sands of Georgia and this same soldier was telling a wonderful tale to his comrades of the great number we killed at Wyatt, as he had gone over the field and seen their graves. Remembering what he had told me about it the day he went over the ground, and thinking maybe he had forgotten it, I said, "Jim, how many graves were there?" "Well, sir," he replied, "I counted one hundred!" This old soldier has long since passed over the river, and I withhold his name. He was a good soldier, but like some men I know now, had no idea of speaking falsely, but had a way of magnifying everything about which he spoke.

I give you now another incident of a different kind in which a boy friend of mine was involved. It occurred not far from Canton, Mississippi and took place as we were marching across an old field in sight of the enemy with the view of flanking them. So soon as we uncovered ourselves in the flanking movement, the enemy began shelling us. The bombs began bursting pretty fast, nearer and still nearer at every discharge, and finally they got our range accurately and having my eyes fixed upon the missiles as they came floating through the air I saw a large bomb before it burst and dodged over on the side of the animal I was riding to escape the fragments when it should explode. I was not touched myself, but my animal was wounded in three places, and a horse just in my rear was disemboweled, and the rider dashed in the dust, and right in my rear as a file leader George Simmons was riding. He was a boy about sixteen, and had never flinched in the face of danger, and had made and continued to make until the end of the war a magnificent soldier. Knowing it was right ticklish times, I glanced back to see how the boys were standing it, when I noticed George Simmons had gotten a little out of line, and was as white as a sheet, and had the appearance of a scared rabbit. I held up my hand and waved it toward him and said, "George, let a thousand men be killed, but nobody scared." He at once became calm and self possessed, and moved back into line, but always said if I had not made the remark I did he would have run!

We were camped at New Albany, Mississippi on the last day of December, 1863, and early in the morning we moved out north toward the Memphis & Charleston railroad, and it was said our objective point was Pocahontas, and the hope of the commander was that we might capture the place. The morning was warm for the time of year, and a slow rain was falling, and this continued until in the evening about three o'clock, when the snow began falling, being carried into our faces by a stiff breeze. We camped for the night just about dark, and then I went with a detail voluntarily about two miles for forage for our mess. It was cold and none of us had seen fire since breaking camp in the morning. Everything we had was soaking wet, and it seemed to me it would be very difficult to build fires, but when we returned with our feed for the horses the boys had a fine blazing logheap fire, and were cooking in soldier fashion. I think that night and the next morning was the most piercing cold weather I have ever felt. Our regiment was in advance the first day and we camped thus at night, but Barteau's regiment⁹ was to take the advance next morning, and as they came up, every man leading his horse, their breath had so frozen on their beards that they presented the appearance of a regiment of ghosts. On consultation it was determined it was too cold to undertake any military movement and we returned to camp, but it took two days to make the return trip and many had frost bitten feet from the cold.

June 8, 1906

The soldier's life is a kind of hum drum dog's life. I have thought that if a man had no business in life, and didn't care whether he ever had or not, and if he had no aspiration in life looking for something better, but was content with what he had, he would be in a very good fix to make a good soldier so far as the mere camp life is concerned. Of course there are higher and nobler qualifications than these to make an ideal soldier, such as fought for the cause of the confederacy during our war in 1861. Take a man though from the common walks of life, as was done in 1861 to 1865, from the plow and shop, the lawyer's office and the mercantile house, the factories and the public employments, and put him to the various and varied duties and employments of a common soldier's life, and he will call it a hard and tough life. In the morning at daylight he must answer to roll call and be ready for an hour's drilling before breakfast, and then go in and cook his breakfast, if he is happy enough to have something to cook. After that he has to hanker around, or sit on a log or his hat, or his saddle if a cavalryman, or lounge on the ground till drilling time again. If the soldier left a home and business requiring his attention or a wife or wife and children, around whom his affections entwine, or quit the fresh turned furrow in the field to attend the call of his country, and thinks of the grass and weeds growing luxuriously where the corn ear should be taking shape and the fleecy staple should look like a beautiful snow bank on the mountain side, his mind turns away from the camp life and a longing for the old scenes takes possession of his affections, and oh! how he wishes to fly away and be at rest in the old home and in the bosom of his family. A lawyer's briefs come crowding up with a new interest, and every little petty case is fraught with a fairy gild, and every old rusty tome is but a leaf from the *Arabian Nights*, or floats before his vision like the chase in Scott's *Lady of the Lake*.

Men in the army are not likely to have a very high appreciation of another man's property, if that property consists of something to eat, does not belong to a fellow soldier, and can be had with tolerable prospects of immunity from punishment. For instance one day while we were on the march in a drizzling December rain, a soldier who had dropped behind came up at a gallop, passing to get up to his company, and an old turkey gobbler was standing by the way and in the soldier's way, all drawed up taking the rain, when the soldier, as he passed, reached over and grabbed the turkey by the wings and never lost a step of the horse, carrying the gobbler along with him for himself and his mess mates for supper that night wherever that might be. I recollect one night one of our men came in after having gone out on a "foraging expedition," bringing back a quarter of mutton. Being asked by one of the boys, "Joe, where did you get that mutton?" promptly replied, "I let no sheep bite me."

When we first went into the army, the commissary was well supplied, and we had more to eat than we could consume, but before the war closed I have seen the men often draw their rations for the day and eat it all at one meal. Let me give you some of the camp drudgery of a soldier's life. Men as a general thing never cook at home unless the cook, be she wife or hired servant, should be sick, and then the little cooking done is nearly of a character "to keep soul and body together," but when you go into the army the men are expected of course as a general thing to do their own cooking, or at least it was so in the war of 1861. Of course there were some men occasionally in the army who had cooks whom they carried from home, being their slaves, and who are now drawing pensions from the state on the same terms that the whites are. The kind of cooking men would do and did do who had never had any experience in that line may well be imagined. Do you wonder there was much sickness among the soldiers when they had to eat such cooking? And think of what a bore it must have been to such men as constituted the rank and file of our army to cook day in and day out through all the long years of the war. And then the vessels in which we cooked had to be washed and scrubbed and often we had to use sand instead of soap with which to clean the vessels. I read of a peculiar rich old man in Australia who always used sand instead of soap in his baths, but was never enabled to appreciate the tale till I saw the sand used on our cooking vessels during the war.

But the worst of it was we had to wash our wearing apparel! Think of a man who had never had any experience in that line moving off to some running brook to wash his clothes, often without soap or fire to heat water! But I want to say to the honor of these men that as a general thing they went about this work in a patient manner and with a cheerful spirit. Some even hilarious, while others carried the calm outward demeanor of dogged persistence, but inward repugnance. We were lined up every Sunday morning for inspection, and every soldier was expected and required to have his gun as bright and shining as a silver dollar, and his accoutrements clean and showy, and woe to the poor fellow who neglected his duty in any of these respects! I never knew why the officers required the inspection to take place on Sunday, unless that and dress parade on Sunday evening was all the work the soldier was required to do on that sacred day.

Another very important, burdensome and often dangerous duty of the soldier was picket duty. The first thing a wise commander did after camping, whether for a night or indefinitely, was to send out pickets on all approaches to the camp. Often it would be pouring down rain, or a drizzling rain, would be falling, and some times the snow would be drifting into our faces, or a regular blizzard would be blowing. No difference what might be the weather, the pickets had to be sent out to protect the camp. It was the duty of the orderly sergeants of the different companies to furnish the details for this duty, and woe on his head if he failed to keep the record correctly! If the wrong man should be put on duty, and especially on one of those cold snowy or rainy nights, and it was discovered, that orderly sergeant would wish he had never had the position.

But the vidette, the sentry posted nearest the enemy to give notice of any approaching danger, had the hardest time of all the pickets. The vidette sentry generally consisted of at least four, if at a pretty dangerous place, one occupying an advanced position to watch for two hours, while the others occupied a position somewhat in the rear, ready to take their turn, or any message to the command which might be necessary. The vidette himself was supposed generally to be stationed at some elevated place to enable him to see an enemy approaching from a considerable distance. On the faithfulness of the picket service depended the safety of the command, and woe to that soldier who should so far forget his duty as to sleep on his post!

Another burden to the soldier was the proper cleaning up of the camp, that it should be kept in a sanitary condition. The efficiency of an army consisted very largely in the health of the men, and their health depended upon the cleanliness of their different camping places. All filth of every kind was required to be burnt or buried, and the soldiers, by detail, were required to do the work.

But to offset these various duties and burdens, there were many things to interest and direct the attention away from the unpleasant things of camp life. You know there are many men who never lack for sources of amusement. There were wags and funny men of the army, ever ready to turn every occurrence to the amusement of the crowd. I remember one day as we were marching along tired and disheartened, when we were ordered to halt and take the side of the road to let the wagon train pass; and as the wagons went by us one by one, all marked "C.S.A."[10] a wag in one of the companies, a mere boy, read out "C.S.A." and then remarked that he "couldn't stand Atlantar"! And so in every strait there was someone ready to direct attention, and help pass off the time.

June 29, 1906

The amusements and diversions by which soldiers passed off the time were many. I remember when we went into camp at Bowling Green, Kentucky, one evening, the boys had much fun catching rabbits. We had had a rather wearisome trip going from Nashville to Bowling Green.[11] When we got to Nashville, there was no chance for any accommodations on the Nashville and Louisville road, the only thing being some inferior freight cars, some boxed and some open. It was cold weather in December, 1861; General Reuben Davis had difficulty in getting any transportation at all. He could not get an engineer at all who had ever run over this road, but was forced to take a new man who had never passed over the road and who was very much averse to making the experiment. But General Davis, who was in command of the troops, pressed him in any way and told him however averse he might be to make the trial he must do it, and thus we made the trip. I am satisfied we made at the rates of a hundred miles an hour in some places owing to the ignorance of the engineer in relation to the road. When we arrived at Bowling Green in the morning tired and sleepy, the ride having been made in the night, there was still delay in getting into camp, and it was in the evening when we were marched into an old field to camp. Soon after we entered the camp the rabbits began jumping up and scudding away across the old field for safety. But the soldiers began pursuing them from behind and hollowing, and heading them off from before, and the little cotton tails became perfectly de-moralized, and gave it up as a bad job to undertake to escape, and would just stop and give up and suffer themselves to be picked up on the ground. In this way our regiment caught forty odd that evening in that camp.

I have also seen the boys on going into a new camp in the woods amuse themselves running squirrels. The noise of the soldiers hol-lowing and running after the squirrels was about as demoralizing to the animals as to the rabbit, but the squirrel had the advantage of going from tree to tree, and he will never give up like the cony.[12] He dies game. But when a regiment of soldiers, and hungry soldiers at that, range themselves over a wood filled with squirrels there is rare fun. The men begin a simultaneous scream, and at the same time running to and fro through the woods, some climbing up the trees, and others with sticks beneath the trees ready to kill the poor fellows so soon as they strike the ground, or even to bat them before they reach the ground. In this way, the wood is soon cleared of squirrels and the men are soon feasting. I have never yet seen a tree with a squirrel up it that some soldier could not climb.

Another amusement was an old fashioned singing bee. When you assemble a regiment of soldiers together, taken as the confederates were from the plow and the office, the shop and the store, we are sure to have some good singers among them, and, some who are leaders at home in that line. Such men generally manage to carry along some song books, as many soldiers did their Bibles. And so at some leisure time, or at night when the stars were shining down on us from a clear sky from above, to see these old singers, some old men some young, gather around a camp fire of blazing logs and hear them sing the old songs of the long ago, was as helpful as diverting. They sang all kinds of songs, from "Hail, ye sighing sons of sorrow" to "Dixie." Sometimes you would hear some one open up round his own camp fire with that old song "Far from the old folks at home" and then you may be sure the boys would collect from all over the camp as soon as the sad wail was heard, and hang with delight on every word and every intonation of the singer's voice till the singing should be over. You can go no place where that old song will not attract and charm. And then the weird old songs of the negro dialect, such as "Way down upon the Swanee river" and "I'm coming, my head am bending low" and so on through the catalogue of old time songs, until some stripling, careless and full of fun and frolic, in order to break the spell, chimes in with "The old Gray horse came tearing through the wilderness," bringing to mind how easily all grave and solemn thoughts can be dissipated. These old time soldier singers did not confine themselves to religious and plaintive airs, but gave their hearers the benefit of love ditties, such as "The Girl I Left Behind Me," or "Annie Laurie," with many more of like kind.

Reading was not a general diversion in the army, for the reason that it was impossible to carry many books, and besides, many soldiers were not readers even at home. Many soldiers carried their Bibles all through the war, and many read them often. I remember to have read my Bible through from Genesis to Revelation in eighteen days and traveled three hundred miles on horseback during the time. Occasionally we would remain long enough at one place for those wishing to read to borrow books of the citizens, and who were always glad to accommodate us in that way.

Another source of amusement and recreation was what I call "piddling." You will always find some out of a regiment assembled together whose bent of mind is for producing some mechanical contrivance for sale and for their amusement. And if you will show me a man of real mechanical genius, I will show you one who can make almost anything on a small scale with a pocket knife and some few other small tools which he can carry in his pocket or saddle bags. Pipe making was one of the amusements by which some passed away the time and made money too. The root of the sour wood, found both in the hills and lowlands of Georgia, furnished excellent material out of which to make a good, beautiful pipe. With an axe to take the root out of the ground and a pocket knife and a small gimlet, the pipe genius was heeled. And I defy the pipe man, whose business it is and always has been to make pipes, to surpass our pocket knife army genius. You see he had at his command time that he did not know what else to do with, and so he kept on marking and carving until he produced a thing of beauty. Then once and awhile you found a "comb" genius. We had a man in our regiment by the name of Carp Mitchell, who always kept a lot of cow's horns on hand, and his small saws, some of which he made himself, and dressing files, and he would make you any kind of comb you wanted, from a common coarse comb to a ladies' cupped side comb, making you a nice fine comb as a yankee could make. I know the old Confederate generally will understand the "modus operandi" by which combs are made from cow's horns; but for the benefit of the younger generation who have not weathered the storm of war, I will state that all you have to do to make a comb of a piece of cow's horn is to saw off a circle as wide as you want the comb, saw it open to one side, boil in water till perfectly soft, then straighten it out altogether, or so much as desired, owing to whether you wish a straight or cupped comb, let it remain pressed out till dry, and then it is ready for sloping for the teeth side, and then for the saw and dressing file.

December 22, 1905

I will this week change the regular course of events, and give my readers a little war incident which I did not myself witness, but the particulars were given me by my brother, J. S. Clayton, one of the actors in the interesting episode.

In the winter of 1864–65, and probably about February of that year, J. S. Clayton and Carroll Mitchener attached themselves to Gambrell's scouts,[13] a kind of independent command, who were at that time hovering round the enemy's outposts a few miles above Memphis, near what is called the "Devil's Elbow" on the Mississippi River. The day after they joined that command, about a dozen of that company planned to make a dash on the pickets of the enemy about five miles east of Memphis. They made the dash, succeeded in capturing the vidette and two horses, and drove the reserve back into Memphis. Carroll and James, my brother, were detailed to carry the captured "Blue Coat" and turn him over to General Forrest,[14] who was then in camp not far from New Albany, Mississippi. After having discharged that duty, they started on their return trip to the "Devil's Elbow" to join their command. On the third night out they stayed all night at Will Tate's, a brother of Dr. Rice B. Tate, who used to live at Mooreville, and with whom both Carroll and James were well acquainted. Will Tate lived near Germantown, Tennessee, as my brother's memory serves him. This was in debatable ground, mostly occupied though by the Federals, yet no harm came to them that night, and next morning they moved on their way, aiming to pass through this town, but, as they approached it, they saw a soldier come out of a house something about a hundred yards to their right, mount his horse and ride towards them, saying, "Come by, boys." He had on a blue overcoat—but many of the Confederates were then in that part of the country—and from his familiar salutation, they supposed he was one of their own men. They left the road and went to meet him. When they had approached to within about thirty feet of him, a ravine being between them, he presented his pistol at brother James, and ordered both of them to hold up their hands. But I want to say that neither of the boys had ever contracted to surrender at even numbers, and much less so when the odds were two to one in their favor. James dropped his bridle reins, raised his left hand as though in fulfillment of the command, but attempted to draw his pistol hung in the scabbard. In the meantime, Carroll, who was about ten feet to the right of James, drew his pistol and fired at the soldier, and he at the same time, having changed his pistol from my brother to Mitchener, fired, both pistols going off at the same time. The shot fired by Carroll cut about one half its depth out of the right cheek of the Federal, while his shot glanced the top of Carroll's hat, a new white one, and scorched and powder burned it somewhat. At this both the Southern boys wheeled their horses, and started back in a run the way they had come, having looked to their right a short distance beheld a large number of cavalrymen coming to the aid of their friend. They demanded the surrender of the boys, but instead of complying they only ran the faster. They ascended a long, slanting hill with the enemy in full pursuit, firing at them constantly. The boys could see their bullets cutting up the dirt at their front making impressions like water falling in a puddle. When they had gone about one half mile, they crossed a bridge, and this delayed the enemy somewhat, but while the boys were going up another long hill, brother's hat blew off. Hats were hats in those days, and he could not get his consent to part with the hat and risk getting another. So when they reached the top of the hill and discovered that only a few of the enemy had crossed the bridge, and that they were about the same distance from the hat as the boys were, James said to Carroll, "I must have my hat!" So they raised the rebel yell, as though they had met their command, and dashed back towards the Federals, yelling, shouting as if they had a dozen or more. They, supposing the Confederates were coming in force, fell back across the bridge, and when the boys reached the hat, still yelling, my brother dismounted and recovered his hat, again mounted and both dashed off for dear life as they had been going. The enemy, seeing the ruse, sent about twenty-five men in hot pursuit. The road was straight for about a mile and a half, and Carroll's horse being rather small and not very fleet, they gained on the boys, and poured the shot into them pretty lively. Coming to a creek, whose bridge had been washed away, and to cross the ford one had to go down the creek about thirty feet, and then come up the channel to near the place where the bridge had been to get out on the other side, my brother, being just then in a considerable hurry, did not go down to the place where the road entered the creek, but jumped his horse off the bank just below the bridge and out on the far side. Carroll, fearing his horse might not be able to cross in this manner, turned up the creek on a road leading in that direction. Four of the enemy followed James, while all the others pursued Carroll, and each could hear the firing at the other for some minutes. Brother, being now untrammeled by a slower horse than his own, gave his horse full rein, and in the course of a mile he had so far distanced his pursuers that they turned back. Desiring to learn what had become of his fellow soldier, he turned to the left, and struck across fields and swamps, intending and aiming to intersect the road he had taken. After the separation Carroll was pursued for about a mile, and being fired on all the time, when he came to a small town, and feeling that his only hope of safety lay in a bold move, adopted the same ruse they had used so successfully in relation to the hat, and again raising a rebel yell, dashed back toward his pursuing foes. He, being hidden just then from the Federals, and they thinking he had surely met up with reinforcements this time, and influenced by the noise he made, fled in great disorder, and their peril was at an end for that time. Carroll, instigated by the same motives which prompted brother James to turn to the left, himself turned to the right, and down in some unknown creek bottom, a mile and a half from any road, and about five miles from their first encounter with the would-be familiar "Blue Coat," the friends met again, and you may be sure no two comrades were ever prouder to see each other than they were. Not a wound had either received, and yet the peril was great, and the escape almost miraculous.

July 7, 1905

Although this article makes me the hero of my own tale, I only make the excuse of Colonel Russell Beene, of old time memory: "He that bloweth not his own horn, it shall not be blown." In December, 1864, the Cavalry Command to which I belonged, being the 12th Mississippi Cavalry, Ferguson's Brigade, was following Sherman through Georgia to the sea.[15] Our orders were to look after stragglers and keep the Federals closed up as much as possible, so as to prevent the burning of property, such as gins, mills, and cotton, not in the immediate path of the army. Many soldiers began to read final defeat between the lines, and squad after squad had dropped out and gone home, so that the disproportion between privates and officers was so great that when we got within something like a hundred miles of Savannah following Sherman, by solicitation of a number of the officers in our regiment, we were detailed as scouts. At the forty-five mile station this side of Savannah, the Federals made a considerable halt, remaining in camp about a week. In the squad to which I was attached were Captain R. H. Allen,[16] and Lieutenants H. W. Bucy and Duke Martin and a private from Texas by the name of Junior, who had gotten lost from his command and fell in with us. We thought we discovered late one evening that the enemy was on the move. We made a dash up close to their camp and captured a prisoner, from whom we learned that the army would break camp the next morning. Early next morning, having sent off the prisoner by Lieutenant Bucy, Captain Allen, Lieutenant Martin and I cautiously examined the situation, and discovered that the Union army was moving on toward the sea. We followed for something like a couple of miles, found the rear guard too strong and too compact to enable us to do them any damage in the way of capturing stragglers. Hoping to follow on later in the day, and have better success, we returned to the camp which had that morning been vacated by the enemy. Captain Allen, who always had a weakness for anything fine or beautiful, having discovered a fine and lovely looking white horse in the deserted camp, which had been abandoned on account of some deficiency in one of his hoofs, was bridling and preparing to place the horse in the care of some residents near the old camp. Lieutenant Martin and I were something like a hundred yards from Captain Allen sitting on our horses in general conversation and especially making some structures on Captain Allen's craze for the one white lame horse. It had been raining that morning, and I had placed my navy in my boot leg under my leggins in order to keep it dry. I had in my lap a repeating breech loading gun which had been captured from the enemy by some of our boys. I myself had become careless, as soldiers will sometimes do, and being wearied with long sitting in my saddle, had kinder stooped over on the horn of my saddle. Lieutenant Martin had only a pistol, and being erect on his saddle, and facing toward the center of the old camp, saw just in front of him and about fifty yards from us two Federal soldiers sitting on their horses and looking at us. Martin said to me, "Lieutenant Clayton, what are those men doing yonder?" I glanced up in the direction he pointed, and saw the two blue coats, and at once hollowed out, "Halt and surrender." But instead of doing so, they started from us in a run, going in the direction their army had gone. Reaching for my pistol, and finding it beneath my leggins, I fired one shot with my repeating rifle while pressing them at full speed. My horse outran Martin's though he pressed with all the vigor and haste possible, his bullets screaming by my ears. One of the men outran the other from the beginning, and showed no disposition to contest the field with us. The other one, very soon after the chase began, dropped his bridle reins, turned as far back square in his saddle as he could, and took deliberate aim at us, but the gun missed fire. Having in the meantime dropped my rifle into my lap and drawn my navy six, I was shooting at the rear soldier as fast as I could, pressing my horse to his speed and gaining constantly on him, and demanding his surrender with every shot. When I had gotten to within about five steps of him, he again squared himself in his saddle and took deliberate aim at my breast. There was no time nor chance to avoid the shot unless by moving more rapidly toward him, and closing my eyes and slapping my spurs to my horse, I dashed onward, heard the snap of his gun again failing to fire, opened my eyes and saw I was a few feet of him, still refusing to surrender, and as a last resort, thought I would be compelled to shoot him through. But for his safety I had shot once too often, my pistol snapped while held in three feet of his back, and knowing I must have discharged all my loads, as I had loaded fresh only that morning, I brought my pistol down with all my power to knock him from his horse, when he sprung a countermine by bringing his gun with all his power upon me, and thus breaking the force of my stroke. Immediately as our weapons clashed, his horse fell dead, shot through in two places, landing the soldier, however, on his feet. Although going very rapidly, I reined my horse at once, threw him well on his haunches, broke one stirrup leather, came near being thrown to the ground, but faced the soldier with my empty pistol presented at his breast, and said "now surrender or I will shoot a hole through you the blackbirds can fly through." I was playing a bluff game, as my pistol was empty. As the collision took place between us, both our guns fell to the ground and were lying at his feet. Seeing the stripes, indicating my rank, he said, "Lieutenant, do not kill me." I told him by no means if he surrendered all right, and this he did, the tears streaming from his eyes. He remarked to me, "you have two very good guns here," pointing to my gun and his, but which he thought were his and his partners. Pointing to my gun, I said, "give me that gun." Thinking he might use the gun on me, I decided if he showed any fight to endeavor to run over him with my horse. But he took the gun by the muzzle and handed me the breech, and as I received it I said, "this is my gun and it is well loaded and I am all right," at the same time slipping a couple of loads also into my pistol. In the meantime Allen and Martin passed on after the other man, but, in the classic language of Captain Allen, "he gathered up his horse with his spurs, shook him well, and was gone like a streak of light."

Now let us turn to another picture. The devotion and constancy of our women to the cause of the South during the war is proverbial, and on the night after the capture of the soldier related above, we had a striking instance of it. Captain Allen went back and brought up his beautiful white lame horse, and deposited him with a resident near the old camp, and we lingered around there through the day hoping to see some soldiers to whom we could deliver our prisoner, so as not to reduce our little force. During the day we made the acquaintance of two families of lonely women residing in the neighborhood, and in about one half mile of each other. All the men of both families were from home serving in the Southern army. We had arranged to remain with our prisoner at one of the houses, and this fact was known to the women at the other house. It was a gloomy December day, the leaden clouds hanging low and bringing darkness early. Soon after dark, and it was a very dark night, the rain began to fall in a slow steady down pour. We had seen no

Federals since the morning, and all our observations let us to believe we were safe for the night and might take the shelter of the good ladies' home, and so we did and had retired, save Captain Allen, who was to be the first to take his turn guarding the prisoner. About ten o'clock, quick steps and a nervous, hurried knock at the rear of the house, indicated danger of some kind. On attending to the call, we had presented to us the familiar faces of two of the young ladies from the other house whose friendship we had made during the day, and who modestly, but excitedly, informed us there were about twenty-five Federal soldiers at their home looking for us, and that they had slipped out the back way, ran through the wood path to warn us of our danger. Not knowing but that the enemy would be coming on the trail of our fair friends, I assure you we lost no time in getting a mile into the woods beneath the great pines, and there on the pine straw without any covering except the over hanging and dripping clouds, we spent the night sleeping soundly, trusting to him who watched to give notice of approaching danger. Next day we turned in our prisoner all right, and pursued our way on track of the advancing enemy, conscious that while we did our duty and showed proper courage we would have the approving smiles and ready assistance of the women of the Southland. We never saw those women, nor the beautiful lame white horse again, but the memory of their devotion to the soldiers of the South held to us through all our perils, and we have looked back to that night and the love of country exhibited by these brave and loyal women, through all these forty years, as a benediction to our lives.

June 22, 1906

It is wonderful how the eve of a battle or fierce skirmish differently affects different soldiers. I remember very well a little incident that occurred just before we went into the fight at a place called the Darby House. It was some distance above Atlanta, and we were covering Johnston's retreat,[17] and holding back the enemy as best we could and as long as we might. We finally found our command, Ferguson's Brigade, just in advance of the Darby House, fronting a superior force and an advancing enemy, consisting of infantry and dismounted cavalry. We threw up the best protection we could out of fence rails and logs, and then awaited the approach of our foe. It was early in the morning when we began the waiting process, the July sun coming over the hillside, stronger and stronger as the delay continued. While we were thus waiting, Lieutenant Jackson was talking to me, together with some others, of his feelings and presentiments about the fight which was coming on, and he showed very clearly that some influence operating on his mind had indicated to him that his days were numbered, and that an enemy's bullet would take him off during the day, and he spoke in a pathetic manner about the loved ones at home, and the improbability of his ever seeing them again on earth. While he was thus giving way to his feelings and lamenting his fate, the Adjutant of the regiment handed me a letter, which I saw at a glance was from my wife from my far away Mississippi home. The balls were then singing occasionally, and our men sending shots in reply at intervals. I did not open the letter, but put it in my pocket intending to read it when the fight was over. The Adjutant said, "Sergeant, why don't you read your letter?" I replied, "I think I shall," throwing the emphasis on the "shall." By this time the fire was pretty constant, and the enemy were advancing slowly but surely. So you can see the difference in my feelings and Lieutenant Jackson's as we were entering into this fight. I could look toward the future and see myself after the battle was over reading my wife's letter, and later realizing the home coming, while poor, noble, brave Jackson saw his own noble form placed in a shallow grave by the foe by whom he had been slain, having only an old Confederate blanket for a winding sheet! But as the enemy advanced, Jackson bore himself as if no future but country and home was in his mind, and was among the last to leave the field. There seemed to have been some mistake made in getting orders to our regiment, and the regiments on the right and left of us both retreated some time before we did. When the order finally came, the enemy were in close proximity to us and pressing with all their vigor. When we got back to our horses just in rear of the Darby residence, the foe were mixing with us, and many of our men had to go out afoot, their horses either getting away from them or being turned loose by the horse holders before they got up. When I got on my claybank, I found myself right by Colonel Inge's[18] side, who, seeing the color bearer with the flag furled, jerked it out of his hands, unfurled it, and hollered, "Fall in, my brave Mississippians, fall in, and face the enemy!" I reined my horse alongside of the Colonel and did all I could to get the boys to stop and form a line in face of the enemy and a galling fire of small arms with bursting shells and screaming shot. But to no purpose. It could not be done. Something like a half dozen stopped, and among the number was Lieutenant Jackson and a young man just merging into manhood by the name of Waller, and a brother to the Adjutant of the regiment. When I saw all hope of rallying the regiment was futile, I waved my hand toward the old field where the men were getting away as fast as they could and best they might and remarked to Colonel Inge, "Yonder go your brave Mississippians, Colonel Inge!" "Then ____ ____, I guess we'd better go too." I remarked to him, "Just as you please about that, sir," and we both moved off following the men. Lieutenant Jackson was just to my right, and when we had moved but a short distance from the Darby House into the old field, the fatal bullet struck him with a thud, the ball evidently entering from behind and shattering the front part of his saddle, as was afterwards seen, where the missile struck after passing through his body. I saw him fall from his horse and saw at once he was dead or dying. But we could not stop to endeavor to render any assistance without being captured, and had to leave our brave comrade to the field of his glory. We lost in killed and wounded at this place forty-three men.

After I had left the death scene of Lieutenant Jackson and had moved some considerable distance across the old field, I overtook John Burdine, a mere boy, who was making his way out afoot as best he could, his mule, which he rode instead of a horse, having gotten away and gone out with the rush. John had his gun, but was very hot and tired. As I came up and he recognized me he said, "Oh, Colonel, let me ride out behind you." The bullets were singing and the bombs bursting all around us, and my old claybank horse was very much excited, as frisky as a four year old. But I said, "John, if you can find any place where you can climb onto my horse, I will carry you out." But stumps and logs there were none thereabouts, and only a few rather small limbs of a tree top lying near. If Burdine had been fresh and having his usual vigor, he could have jumped up behind me very readily from the limbs I have mentioned. But being well run down and exhausted, he made a rather weak effort at a spring and kinder caught hold of me with one hand while one foot was partly thrown over the horse, and thus swinging the horse made a quick turn, the saddle turned and brought John, me, and the saddle all off! But I swung on to the bridle and thus held the horse. Having readjusted the saddle amid the falling of bombs and the singing of balls, and with difficulty again mounted, I said, "Now, John, come here to this log, which I think is a little larger, and make a big jump and I'll carry you out." But the horse was so frisky, the log so small and Burdine so tired, that the second effort to mount him behind me failed as the first, but more disastrous still, as by his effort he carried me and the saddle again from the horse's back, but this time the animal jerked loose from me, kicked the saddle from him and went out with the onrushing tide on to the Confederate side. So John and I were left on an equality, except that his mule had carried out his saddle and mine was left behind. Passing on myself for some distance, thinking to leave everything with the enemy, I bethought me that all of my wearing apparel and blankets to keep me warm were lost, and that a man might well risk his life for articles so valuable. I retraced my steps and gathered up my saddle bags containing my wearing apparel and one good blanket, and left the rest for lost for all time to come. But I made a friend that would stick to me like a brother. If I should now require help of any kind in the power of John Burdine, and who now lives in Smithville, in Monroe county, Mississippi, he would fly to my rescue on the wings of the wind and every sorrow of mine receives a returning throb from his big heart and sympathetic nature.

July 6, 1906

I only remember one time during the war that I felt a kind of presentiment that I would be shot, and that was conditional. On the day before the fight at Atlanta, which I think was on the 22nd of July, 1864, we were holding the enemy in check as best we could, and they were pressing us back as fast as they could. We built the best breastworks we could for our protection, and they were generally constructed of rails and logs. That morning after having been pushed back several times, we built a very good temporary work for our protection on the slant of a beautifully wooded hill near the outskirts of the city, and hoped we would not be compelled to evacuate any more that day. But we were doomed to disappointment. The Federals came on with a rush, and something impressed me that I would be shot if I fell back as the others did, but the thought came to me that I would be safe if I should wait till the first volley should be drawn and then make a break. Acting on this suggestion, I remained behind the protection when the order to retreat came until the first fire was given, and then moved out as rapidly as I could after my command, when the bullets flew so thick round my head that I felt like the whole yankee army were firing at me. Still I came out without a scratch, and our regiment went out in good style, and the brigadier general of our command[19] came round and publicly commended Colonel Inge for the manner in which his troops conducted themselves. So soon as the balance of the brigade had somewhat gathered in place, an order came for men in charge of an officer to properly locate the position of the enemy and make reports to General Ferguson, but under no circumstances to fire a gun. I was placed in charge of the detail and very soon and very readily located the position of our foes, and the temptation was strong indeed to shoot some of them. Being confident that they had so demoralized us by their last move on our breastworks that we would not be ready for some time at any rate to make another stand, they had become careless and were scattered about in an old peach and apple orchard eating the fruit, climbing the trees and paying but little heed to their own safety, and offered a very tempting target for our guns, and we were close enough for each man to have made a telling shot. But a soldier knows his duty and we could only find out and report and must not shoot. It was only a short while after this that they found out where we were, and they not having the same orders in relation to shooting which we had, we felt the effect of their lead. At this place Lieutenant Hale and James Cornathan were both wounded, one being next to me on the right and the other on the left and they were struck almost at the same time, and yet I did not feel like I would be hit, as I did in the morning when leaving the rail pile breastworks.

After Sherman began his march through Georgia to the sea, our command was ordered to follow in his rear and hang on his flanks so that his command might be kept in as close and compact body as possible. The more ground the enemy spread over the more damage he would do. I think from my observations on this trail that this command had very liberal foraging orders. They took every hog, cow, sheep, goat and all horses and mules, together with all poultry; burnt every gin and mill anywhere in reach and destroyed all cotton; carried off and destroyed together all grain of every kind and even dug the sweet potatoes from the ground or took them from the banks where the farmers kept them. I have heard it said the Federals were commanded to respect the household goods of the citizens. Well, may be so; but to a man right on their heels, seeing, as we did, it seemed more like an order to enter the houses and despoil them of every thing they owned than to respect their rights. Of course the soldiers could not carry off everything, but we were in many houses where very little was left even in the way of bedding and household property. As for leaving anything to eat, that was not done as a rule. After we had been following Sherman some time, our companies were so depleted of man "home goers" that a scout of officers was made at their request, and detached from their respective commands. After some time we became separated, and for a time Captain Bob Allen, Lieutenant Duke Martin, and I were together, and finally Martin fell out on account of sickness and Allen and I were left alone of the detail, having with us a private from Texas by the name of Junior. After having captured and turned over a soldier one day, we again followed on as near to the enemy as we well could, and being right in the wake of the army's desolation we had a good chance to see what damage was done. I could see very readily why they should wish to destroy all our cotton and carry off all beef cattle, hogs and sheep and the horses and mules which could be used by our army, but why they should wish to burn every little water mill in the country passes comprehension, except on the theory that they wished war to appear as near hell as possible. And then when they went so far as to break up the little family hand mills, the very height of meanness was reached. I can better illustrate to you what desolation was made by telling some incidents which came under our own observation on this trip. Some time toward the middle of December 1864, Captain Allen, Private Junior and I put up at the house of an old man whose farm had been raided and desolated by the enemy. He was something over seventy. His boys were all in the confederate army, save those who had fallen in her cause. He and his old help mate of many years were living alone. He had a fine plantation and about thirty slaves, plenty of stock, and a good supply of provisions and all needed household goods. Having heard before the Federals came that they were destroying all mills and gins, and having a nice old time hand mill for grinding corn, he got his negroes to carry the mill off into the woods and hide it, hoping to save it so he could grind a little meal for himself and wife when the mills should all be destroyed. We rode up just at night and asked to be housed for the night. Learning we were Southern soldiers he was very willing to do anything for us in his power, "but" said he, "the yankees have ruined me. I have nothing for you to eat except some sweet potatoes, a few of which they left me. It is the only morsel I have to eat. I have gathered up a few bushels of corn left on the ground by the enemy, and that I want to grind on my hand mill to make bread for the old woman and me till we can do better, and in the morning I want you men to help me bring my hand mill from the place where I hid it, as it is too heavy for me to handle. You are welcome to sleep in my beds, though they have left me but little, and you can gather up corn where they have wasted it on the ground for your horses." The old man seemed very much crushed and I remember a conversation we had with him that night in which I felt very much like the Texas Junior ought to have been severely reprimanded. The old man had been telling us what he had, only leaving him the few potatoes and the little pile of corn he had gathered up and Captain Allen's heart and mine were bleeding in sympathy when Junior clipped in with "Eh! old man that's nothing. Above here they are living on herbs, and roots and acorns." The old man replied in a very sad manner, "Ah young man, it might not be much to you. But it's every thing to me." Next morning, having made our supper and breakfast of roasted potatoes and being ready to depart, the old gentleman said, "now men you must go and help me bring in my hand mill from its hiding place." We went with him to the hiding place of the mill only to learn the vandals had been there before us, and broken it into many pieces. The old man's sad countenance and tearful eyes, as he looked upon the broken mill, will cling to me while the years last.

July 13, 1906

On leaving the old Georgia farmer who was ruined by the Federal army, as detailed in our last article, Captain Allen and I, accompanied by Private Junior of Texas, moved on toward the rear guard of the enemy hoping to pick up some stragglers. I give you in detail another little incident illustrative of the utter destruction of the country. It will enable you to more readily understand what I mean by the condition of the country than any words I might use. Moving on a short distance from our old host of a night, we passed a farmhouse by the roadside and stopped to make some inquiries, and found the dear women anxious to tell of their ruin and desolation. They spoke of the fact that the army of invasion had burned all the mills everywhere at all in reach, rendering it impossible for them to get any corn ground into meal. I noticed while we were listening to the women that someone had turned over a large ash gum full of ashes. It was an immense concern, so large it could not be replaced without taking all the ashes out of it. After telling of her utter ruin and desolation, she fixed her eyes on the old fallen gum as it lay in its wreck and ruin, like the hulk of some old ship stranded on the shore, and while the tears came to her eyes, she said, "But, I could have done better if they had left me my ash gum!" To you this may seem laughable, as it did to me at the first. But what she meant was that by the destruction of her ash gum the enemy had deprived her of the means of making lie hominy,[20] the staff of life where no mills existed. When I came to think of it in that light I felt that it was really a pathetic scene. No one can tell what an ash gum could be to a poor woman having nothing to eat but a little corn and no mill on which to grind it. The men of this home were in the Southern army fighting for what they conceived to be their rights, while woe and want stared their women in the face. Such women, I think, deserved to see their sons and husbands come home conquerors. But while this could not be, they came as heroes, and their heroism is the common heritage of the whole country.

Right here I think a proper occasion to say something of Captain R. H. Allen. I never knew Captain Allen till during the war and when I first saw him it was in Tupelo and in 1863. He was quartermaster for Colonel Inge's Regiment of Cavalry. Afterwards he was captured and remained in the hands of the enemy till some time in the fall of 1864. When he came back to his command his place was filled by another and he, not being anxious to find a bomb proof position, shouldered a gun and buckled on a pistol and went to the front. In the midst of danger he was calm and self possessed, never losing his head, as the saying goes, and never finding the man or set of men whom he was afraid to face at odds. I have been with him when the circumstances were such as to try men's souls and I always found him true as steel. I remember an incident or two which occurred wherein he acted his part well and fearlessly when our friend Junior was with us, of whom I have spoken heretofore.

One evening rather late we three rode up to a place where a depot had been before Sherman passed but which was then minus the depot building and the railroad was a wreck. When we rode up everything looked like the moles and bats had taken possession of the place, except that one lone white man was standing there. He

looked very lonesome, but was of military age, and if we had been
in some other place and at some other time, we might have made
some inquiries of him along that line, but as it was, we had not time
for that. He looked very much like he was all the man in the world
and that no women were ever expected to make their appearance in
all the coming years. We rode up in a hurry and I said in my short
and blunt way, "Have you seen any Yankees here lately?" "Yes,"
was his answer. "How long since, and which way did they go?" was
my rejoinder. "Only a short while and they took that road," pointing to a settlement road leading to the left from the railroad and the
main road. No one gave any order. I said nothing to either Captain
Allen or Private Junior, nor did either of them speak to me. I very
well knew that Captain Allen wanted to see his foe, and as for
Junior, neither Captain Allen nor I had the utmost respect for him
since we heard him speak so lightly of the old farmer man's distres-
ses, and besides that, in a charge we had made a few days before in
which we captured some federals, Junior made the Yankee he first
got to deliver up his pocket book and contents. So by common
consent we struck out at a sweeping gallop down the byroad the
lone man pointed out as the one the enemy had gone. If you have
your enemy with his back to you and can thus take him in the rear
and unaware, the course we then took is all right; but to rush on
your foe thus when he is fronting you and aware of your approach
is not good generalship unless you have taken the precaution to
ascertain his position and strength. In this instance my idea was to
overtake the soldiers who had just left the old burnt depot before
they got back to their command. We had found from experience if
we could make a rush on stragglers we rarely failed to make a
capture. The enemy were moving on several different roads all con-
verging on Savannah, and they kept up constant communication
between the different highways by means of the country or private
ways. These men who had just been down to the main road at the
depot, and who had been pointed out to us by the lone way farer I
have mentioned, were evidently a part of a larger detail whose
business it was to keep up this communication between two of the

routes on which Sherman was moving. The country was a beautiful level wooded plain, and we made no halt for anything, but kept up our gallop for about one-quarter of a mile, when we saw just in front of us and about one hundred and fifty yards away a company of about twenty-five men. Seeing the number and knowing we could not effect anything by charging them, but being of the opinion they would think we were surely supported by a larger command or we would not have ventured so near, we dismounted and each man held his own horse while we poured hot shot into them for some little time with our repeating rifles. We either killed or badly wounded one man, whom his comrades carried to the rear in full view. Having stayed as long and probably a little longer than was prudent, Captain Allen suggested we had better retire. I fully agreed with him, and we moved back in the direction from which we came and to the main road where we left the lone stranger. When we returned to the depot place, where ruin and desolation reigned, and saw the ascending smoke of the recent fires of the enemy, the lone stranger still stood like a wandering Arab looking on the wreck of his home land.

July 27, 1906

Passing the lone pilgrim mentioned in my last article, standing by the old burnt depot, without time to make an inquiry or to answer a question if it had been asked, we moved down the main road, following the trail of Sherman's army at a sweeping gallop, hoping to capture some stragglers who had fallen behind. We moved on this way for about one half mile, when we halted for consultation. We had gotten near the camps of the enemy. All in to the left of the road we could hear them cutting wood, hollowing and singing songs. On the right of the road at the place we stopped for consultation there was what the people of that country call a bay, but which we would here call a deep wooded swamp. It was mostly of sourwood growth, and there was a shallow branch running through it, and the swamp was quite boggy. At the place where the stream ran across the road, it had spread out several yards wide, but only six inches to a foot deep. We stopped for consultation just on the north side of the water. Captain Allen and I were in favor of creeping up and watching a chance to sweep down on some stragglers, rush them into the bay or swamp on our right, thread our way back north through the woods, and thus save ourselves and our prisoners. Private Junior thought prudence was the better part of valor, and was decidedly in favor of retreating at once by the way we came, kept himself well to our rear, and made strong protests against moving another step forward.

Allen and I in the meantime as we talked, had moved across the water of the bay at the road, and Junior had gone about half way over, when we saw two Federals about one hundred and fifty yards in advance of us trudging slowly along the road, evidently tired and footsore. They had never seen us, and had no idea there was an enemy anywhere near, and we pointed out to Junior the ease with which we could rush on them and pick them up and rush into the swamp with them, but he wheeled his horse and started back north, making a great splatterment of water, accompanied with considerable noise. Seeing Allen and I did not follow his movements, he hesitated. I said to Captain Allen. "Bob, that fellow is not going with us, but is scared almost to death; suppose we try those yankees ourselves and let him go. There are only two of them and two of us and we will have the rush on them." "All right," said Allen, but just at that moment Junior made another bigger splatterment in the water with his horse and our attention was directed for a moment toward him, and when we again fixed our eyes on the road and our straggling yankee soldiers, we glanced our eyes about one hundred yards in advance of them and saw three more soldiers in advance of their comrades. Bob and I would have been willing to have rushed on the five if Junior had been one of us, but as it was, he not only refused to go with us, but moved to the rear. I said again, "Bob, I hardly think we should tackle all five unless Junior would accompany us. What do you say?" He replied, "You're right, but we must stop that fellow and bring him under command." About that time Junior hollowed out, "Men come on, or we will be captured," and started to move right back the way we had just come. I then sternly and indignantly ordered him to halt and fall into our rear, and we moved at once into the swamp instead of back the road we had just come, and from which direction we very well knew the enemy were coming if at all. The swamp was so thickly set with undergrowth and the ground so soft we had difficulty in getting any distance into the bay, when we heard the federal soldiers come down the road we had just left. From the noise they made and the conversation they had we judged there were about twenty-five of them, and they were cursing the "D——d Johnnies" for the move we had made on them, causing them to have to leave their camp after stopping time. I had a very frisky claybank horse, and the mud was soft and deep, and he would move about while we were waiting for the enemy to pass and jerking his foot and leg out of the mud, it would make a noise almost equal to the noise of a rifle, and it almost frightened Junior out of his wits, and he said in a whisper, "My God, Lieutenant, your horse will betray us," while Captain Allen sat there on his horse as calm and serene as if on dress parade, with the faintest smile playing over his countenance, with features set for a conflict, and a manner that said plainer than words, "Clayton, whatever comes I am with you to the death." But as luck would have it, or as God intended it, as you will, they passed on without discovering our hiding place.

When the yankees passed, Junior seemed much relieved indeed, and I must say I breathed more freely myself and felt as though I had more elbow room. Captain Allen and I decided we would try our hand at woodcraft in leaving our concealment, until we should get well out of our enemy's camp. The sun was just casting his last rays over the forest as we entered it. In every swamp specially adapted to the purpose and in every wooded ravine near any residence, we found boxes and trunks broken open and the contents carried off. Often the people did by their household goods as our farmer friend did by his handmill for grinding corn, got the negroes to hide them out, and then when the enemy came they would point out to them the hiding place of the trunks and boxes, and they never failed to go into all such hidden articles. They sometimes left what was in the house, or a part of it, but that which was hidden was doomed to destruction.

At another time when we had a rather full attendance of officers on the scout, Captain Allen being along, we found a considerable squad of Federals pillaging at a farmhouse. They made fight, and while the officer in command rather hesitated to charge for a moment, shooting at them at long range, they wounded Captain G. W. Walker in the arm. But our hesitation was only for a moment, and we then charged and captured several of the enemy. When we got back to a camping place the question was how we should manage to get the ball out of Captain Walker's arm, it having entered somewhat above the wrist and come near the surface on the upper outside of the arm, about four inches from the shoulder. We had no surgeon with us and no doctor in the country. My friend Captain Allen was not at all averse to blood-letting when his enemy was involved, but he could not cut and carve a friend. We had no one there who had ever seen chloroform administered to unconsciousness. I knew there was danger in it, for only a few months before, the doctors had put a poor fellow under the influence of it to cut a ball out of his back, he being well and hearty, and he never waked up anymore. But it seemed necessary to do something, and so I said, "Captain Walker, if we can get some chloroform at this house, and you are willing to let me administer it, I will do so and cut that ball out." To this he agreed. We got the chloroform and I called for a razor, and asked the assistance of some of the boys, and applied the chloroform. Never having seen it applied, and not knowing just how it would affect anyone, and also being fearful of giving too much, I stopped when he got to preaching right well, and said, "Give me that razor and hold him and I will cut out the ball, chloroform or no chloroform." In the trial and investigation of the first murder case I had ever defended, I had learned that the large arteries were on the inside of the limbs. So, remembering this, and determining to cut as near straight up and down with the arm as possible, I made the incision rapidly, while the captain was in the midst of his preachment, and lifted out the ball and bound up the wound and sent the captain on for a furlough; but the war closed before he recovered sufficiently to return. But the thought of a poor fellow being wounded so far away from home and wife and loved ones and no tender hand to smoothe his brow, but rough, uncouth men alone to administer to his wants, and an unskilled cobbler to cut and slash on his wounded form, was too much for Captain Allen's sympathetic nature, and the tears unbidden flowed. When we, however, reflect again how many poor fellows died on neglected fields, or in far off prisons, with no loving wife or devoted mother to wipe the death damp from their brows, nor to carry any loving message they might wish to send to the vine clad hills or lovely valleys of the Southland, we hold up our hands in horror, and say Sherman was right when he said, "War is hell." Let us ever give a "God speed you" to those who are interesting themselves in universal peace for the nations.

August 3, 1906

When Christmas of 1864 came, even the average Southern soldier could begin to see the "handwriting on the wall," and many, thinking of the ruin which was already wrought and of the certainty of the end, and fixing their minds and hearts on the wife and children in the homeland, were led to leave their commands and go home. And many a strong and vigorous man who remained with his command, looked up to the God of battles and cried for help and relief; and many a night, amid the pine forests of Georgia and the Carolinas, brave men, but whose hearts were bleeding for their country and their homes, sought the God who rules the destinies of men, and cried mightily for deliverance—some way, any way—that would restore them to their homes and loved ones and still give them freedom. But when the news was spread abroad in our camp that the brave and chivalrous Lee had been compelled to surrender his brave men, strong and brave men cried like children. It is true we had been looking through the many coming months at the cordon of increasing soldiers drawing nearer and still nearer, and viewing the mighty oncoming hosts—coming, coming and ever coming more and more, while our little band was decimated and none to fall back on or draw from at home, the boys of sixteen having entered the service—yet it was so hard to believe the gallant Lee must be the first of the great commanders to surrender to the enemy. But even then, a soldier is so true to his cause, we did not say much to each other about the cause being utterly lost. We thought that even after Lee had surrendered,[21] we might succeed, and I must say that it did not enter my mind that we were on the eve of the close of the war till Johnston gave up the fight.[22] Then all at once it dawned upon me that the war was over, and an intense longing came over me to see the loved ones at home. We were at Rock Hill, South Carolina when our commanding general received the news of Johnston's surrender, but he kept it from the command until we got to Washington, Georgia, and we then received the news by the printed protocol coming into our hands. General Ferguson seemed to be anxious to march us through the country and cross over to the Trans-Mississippi Department to still carry on the war. For several days before we came to Washington, Georgia, we had been in the train with the fleeing President of the Confederacy, and at that place his treasurer distributed to each soldier and officer alike twenty-five dollars in specie.[23]

I was in command of our regiment when the time came to surrender our forces, and I received "Parol," as we then called it, and was given authority to issue like papers to the men, and all of Inge's regiment who were with the command at that time had a parol from me. I saw one of them not long ago. I remember very well when we went to the Federal post to surrender and receive our papers, the yankee commander did not know how to write them. He was very willing we should surrender but he did not understand how to frame the writing. Colonel Broyles, of the 56th Alabama Cavalry, said, "Give me the pen and paper and I will write it." He was a man about forty, as I would judge, and a lawyer, and taking in his hand the cartel which Sherman and Johnston had entered into, and it was only a short while till the Colonel had written a paper satisfactory to the Federal officer, and which all the commanders of regiments copied and used. After I had given my men their parols, I told them I of course had no further authority over them, but that if they wished to remain together, and would conduct themselves like good, law abiding citizens, and pay for what they should get for themselves and their horses, I would see that they were provided for till they got home. The thought came to me that it might be necessary at some stage of the route to impress something to eat or for forage for our horses, and I thought it would be better to have a kind of head for that purpose. This the men all agreed to. We had as much "domestic"[14] as we could carry on our horses, which the people would be glad to receive for rations and forage in addition to our twenty-five dollars in silver. We got along very well till about the third night, when we were refused forage for our horses. The gentleman had ample, but refused to let us have it on any terms. We offered him domestic or silver, as he might choose. He was an Alabama mountaineer, and did not wish to accommodate a Southern soldier. We used all the argument we could bring forward to no avail. It was then dark, and a long distance to the next house, and our horses were fagged out. I had told the men if they would act right and pay for all they got, I would see that they were provided for. After the gentleman had refused us anything on any terms, I told him we would be compelled, as much as we regretted it, to take enough of his corn to feed our stock, and that the money—silver money—was ready to pay for it. No, he would receive nothing, and besides that he would have us all in jail before morning. But we had no idea of going to prison, but took his corn and went into camp. It was not very long until the gentleman cooled down and came around and got his pay.

I remember very distinctly that the nearer I got to my home the fewer of us remained together as every fellow branched off at the proper place for his home until I was left alone. I was riding an ambulance mule, my horse—the gallant old clay—having died at a place called the "Devil's half acre" in Georgia. I made over sixty miles the last day, and come in the back way on the 18th day of May. I placed my feet upon the door step of the little cabin in my father's yard where my wife and little girl were staying during my absence; and although I had not been at home for over a year, so soon as my foot struck the entrance my wife called my name, but the little girl, almost two years old, knew me not. What a sad and desolating thing is war that it keeps the young children from knowing their parents! When I landed at home I was very much nonplussed to know what to follow. Had no cotton planted and the corn was about laid by, and a wife and child to support and only twenty-five dollars on hand. Very soon, however, the little cotton still in the country began to move toward the market, and having one good mule and my father furnishing one and a wagon, I concluded to follow wagoning for a time until the courts should open up. So I made one trip to Cherokee on the Tennessee river, two trips to Memphis, carrying two bales of cotton each trip and dividing the money I received therefor with my father. I had contracted to make the third trip to Memphis when I went over to Fulton and learned the legal business was opening up, when I got my brother Thomas to carry the load, and I again moved to Fulton and entered upon my life work at the law.

June 9, 1905

Often in the olden days, and on down through the years which have come and gone, I have passed the grave of an old Arkansas soldier resting silently and quietly beside the public highway on the Tupelo and Fulton road, out in old Itawamba county. For many years, while Baxter McFarling was chancellor of this district, we went together generally from Tupelo to the Chancery Court at Fulton, and always as we approached the grave of this old soldier, the chancellor would say, "Here's the old soldier, and we give him honor," and we both invariably raised our hats, and often spoke of the lone grave, the thoughtfulness of the road hands, who at intervals renewed the enclosure round the grave, and of the probability or improbability of his homefolks knowing where he was resting all these years. After Bragg's army fell back to Tupelo from Corinth, there being much sickness in the army,[25] a brigade of General Price's command moved out into the piney woods, about a fine spring, just north of the last resting place of this old soldier, and there, amid the lonely pines of old Itawamba, far away from the old home in Arkansas, surrounded only by his companions in arms, and with no loving mother, darling wife, or precious sister to wipe the death damp from his brow, or even to offer a prayer for his passing soul, he breathed his last, and was buried by the road-side;

and now, and through all these years, and on down through the coming ages, the everlasting moans of the pines have sung, are now singing, and shall always sing his requiem. It seems to us that it was very unfortunate for this old soldier's loved ones that he was not buried in some church yard cemetery; for I notice that when the flowers of May and June come in all their loveliness and beauty, the survivors of the lost cause, and their mothers and daughters, and the sons and daughters of the confederacy, annually meet to do honor to their dead heroes by scattering flowers on their graves, while the last resting place of this old Arkansas soldier receives no attention. But I am glad of one thing—nature make no invidious distinctions. The eastern sunbeam glistens in the dew drop that clings to the sprig of grass growing by his side, and the grass grows as luxuriantly, and the wild flowers bloom as sweetly, and the stars shine with the same brightness, and the moon sends down the same mellow light, and the rain descends as softly and gently, and the beautiful snow gives its covering of white, as if his grave by the wayside were the mausoleum of a prince. And the Great Father of light and love, watches his dust as carefully, and with as much interest, as if a Washington or a Lincoln were buried there.

Often as I have lain awake on my bed in the "wee sma' hours of the morning," I have thought of this old soldier's grave, and the thought has come into my mind, "Somebody's darling lies buried there by the roadside." Then my mind has flown away to the valleys of Arkansas, and rested upon an humble cottage country home upon a little hillock, where the wild flowers bloom and where the surroundings indicate that the inmate is poor. And in my mind's eye, I have looked into that little cottage, and there found a widowed mother, who, when I first thus saw her many years ago, was past fifty, with a kind and motherly look, tall and noble in bearing, beautiful shaped hands, raven black hair, slightly touched with silver, a dark, dreamy eye, form somewhat stopped with sorrow and care, with a smile on her face that was a benediction to the whole neighborhood. Before the war came to send sorrow and woe to so many hearts, I have imagined that the husband had passed over the river, and the soldier boy, whose grave I have pointed out, was her only support, comfort and hope. How fondly she clung to him, and how hopefully she looked up to him to fill his father's place as her stay and support, and to provide a home for himself, where she too might always be an inmate, as happy as a widowed mother might be. But before her fond hopes had been realized, the war trumpet sounded its blast, and, with the true, patriotic love of country so characteristic of Southern chivalry, the boy, the only boy of the widowed mother, called for his mother's blessing in order to join the Southern army. None but a mother can tell how hard it is to send forth an only son to fight for his and her country. But with the devotion to country so specially exhibited by our Southern women during the Civil war, she gave him her benediction, telling him to ever sustain the honor of the standard, even if it should result in his death and separation from her for all time to come. And when he had gone, methinks after every battle, she might be seen looking for and asking of everyone passing her humble home as to the safety of her darling boy. And finally, when the sad news was broken to her that her soldier boy had died and been buried in Mississippi soil, but for the sustaining grace of the Father above she could not have survived the shock. And since then and through all these years, as I have been passing the grave of her dead soldier boy, she has been bowed down with grief and sorrow for the lost and the loved. And as I myself, an old soldier now, have ridden by her boy's last resting place, and have allowed my mind to meditate upon his probable mother, I have seen in vision, or dream, or mind's eye picture, this devoted mother ever and anon, glancing round, or turning toward the door of her humble home at the least noise, or looking over her glasses at the oncomers, as though she were still looking for her Willie to come home again even after all these years.

I suppose I take more interest in this old soldier's resting place than most others do, because always when I pass his grave, and think of his loved ones, and of his lonely death, so far away from home and loved ones, my mind flashes over the space and rests upon the sandy beach of Fernandiana, where amid the sand of Florida, and beneath the ever moaning pines of that lonely beach, rests the body of my own dear brother soldier boy Charlie. And I well remember and shall never forget the anguish of my mother's heart when she heard of his death, and how, for almost thirty years, she mourned his loss, and with what loving tenderness she handled that last letter which he wrote her, and how fondly she read it over and over again through all those eventful years. And oh! when I think of these, and paint their pictures in these pages, both as to soldiers and mothers, I have painted you the picture of the Southland, her dead soldiers and her living loved ones.

NOTES

[1] Obviously Clayton.

[2] Sir Walter Scott's *The Lay of the Last Minstrel.*

[3] By Alexander Beaufort Meek.

[4] Maj. Gen. Sterling Price commanded Confederate troops in Mississippi, Arkansas, and Missouri from March 1862 to the end of the war.

[5] Tooth-Picks, Rangers and Cowboys, and Tigers and Zenaves are Confederate military units.

[6] Maj. Gen. George Edward Pickett advanced his small division unsuccessfully against the Federal center at Gettysburg on July 3, 1863, in the famous "Pickett's charge."

[7] Robert E. Lee, General in Chief of the Armies of the Confederate States, and Maj. Gen. Thomas Jonathan "Stonewall" Jackson, both natives of Virginia.

[8] This could have been a small skirmish, or Clayton has mistaken the date of this engagement. Confederate records show that Clayton's unit fought at Collierville, Tennessee, on October 11-12, 1863.

[9] Col. C. R. Barteau's command included the 12th Mississippi Battalion of Cavalry, of which Clayton was a member.

[10] Confederate States of America.

[11] In the fall and winter of 1861, a contingent of Mississippi troops led by Maj. Gen. Reuben Davis was sent to Bowling Green, Kentucky, to hold Southern fortifications for a brief period.

[12] Rabbit.

[13] Formed of men from Itawamba County, Mississippi.

[14] Lieut. Gen. Nathan Bedford Forrest commanded Confederate cavalry in north Mississippi and west Tennessee.

[15] In the fall of 1864, the 12th Mississippi Cavalry was transferred from the command of Brig. Gen. Samuel Wragg Ferguson to that of Gen. Joseph Wheeler, and fought in several engagements with Union troops commanded by Maj. Gen. William T. Sherman during his infamous march to the sea from Atlanta to Savannah.

[16] Allen apparently joined Clayton after being captured by Union forces in May, 1863, during the Tupelo campaign. He was held in Federal prisons in Illinois, Virginia, and Maryland before being released in the spring of 1864.

[17] Gen. Joseph E. Johnston commanded Confederate armies that opposed Sher-

man on his march from Chattanooga to Atlanta in the late spring and summer of 1864.

[18] Capt. William M. Inge, commander of the 12th Battalion of Mississippi Cavalry.

[19] Ferguson.

[20] Actually, lye hominy. The grains of corn were soaked in a weak lye solution, made with the wood ashes.

[21] April 9, 1865.

[22] April 26, 1865.

[23] The 12th Battalion of Mississippi Cavalry was part of the cavalry escort of Confederate States' President Jefferson Davis from Charlotte, North Carolina, to Washington, Georgia, where Davis ordered that silver coin brought from Richmond, Virginia, be disbursed to the troops as partial pay.

[24] Confederate currency.

[25] Gen. Braxton Bragg took command of the Confederate Army of Tennessee in June 1862 at Tupelo, Mississippi, where 18,000 of an 80,000-man army became sick from drinking foul water.

CHAPTER V

"Not A Good Wagon Mule to Be Found. . ."

THE AFTERMATH OF WAR: 1865–1875

Just what was heaped upon a proud and noble people here in the South after the war, none will ever know after this generation passes off the stage of action.

THE THREE ARTICLES in this chapter are valuable documents of social history. They show the deep bitterness of the white Southerner at the treatment in defeat of "a proud and noble people." On a more complex level, Clayton also articulates, perhaps without even realizing it, the strong feelings of betrayal at what he perceives as the disloyalty of freedmen to their former masters. His attitude toward the freed blacks is ambivalent. He sees them, on the one hand, as recalcitrant children being led astray by crafty outsiders; on the other, he views blacks with aversion and bitterness, questioning their capacity to act intelligently in positions of leadership.

Although Clayton's focus is on the problems of the white Southerner during the Reconstruction, what emerges indirectly in this chapter is also a sense of the many crushing pressures exerted upon the Southern black after the Civil War. Handicapped by illiteracy and little knowledge of the ways of the world, the ex-slave finds himself at the mercy of the avaricious scalawag, the resentful white Southerner, and both Republicans and Democrats who seek to manipulate him politically.

In this chapter, then, the roles during the Reconstruction of both the Southern white and the Southern black seem almost untenable. Neither is free. Both are under intense pressure. Both emerge as victims.

November 30, 1906

When the war of 1861 had closed and the survivors of the army returned to their homes, they found many changes had taken place in their absence, and especially was this noticeable in the border land of the country. In the first place, all property in slaves was destroyed, and the supply of horses and mules had been reduced very much. Such a thing as a good saddle horse or a good wagon mule could not be found, unless they had been hidden out, and this was a very dangerous thing to do. Some enemy or slave would be almost sure to point out the hiding place of the stock, and if the enemy came, he took them, and if the friend happened along, he impressed them for service, and in either event, the stock was gone and the owner none the better off, as the scrip given by the friend proved of no more value toward the last than the want of it by the enemy. To the everlasting credit of the negroes it must be said that they were so far loyal to their owners as a general thing that they remained at home and worked faithfully, and in many instances had the care and possession of the entire interests of their master's farms and stock, and were ever ready to do and suffer whatever might be required for the interest of their owners.

After the war in all the thinly settled slave districts, like North Mississippi, they still remained at home and finished the crops before they were turned loose as free. I have often thought that as the slaves assembled round the cabin hearths in the days succeeding the close of the war and before the time of their final release, they had wonderful reasonings among themselves as to what would be the outcome of the war to them. You must remember that they could neither read nor write, and only in a few instances had anyone explained to them that Lincoln had issued his proclamation freeing them, and as we went on with our work as formerly, they must have endeavored often to peer into wonderland to find what it would bring to them. And yet how cautious they must have been, because of the fear of punishment. They had not yet learned that they were no longer in fear of the Patrolers if they failed to carry a pass from their owners, and consequently had not moved about much. I remember very well that our slaves were just as obedient and worked as well during the making of the crop of 1865 as they had ever been and done. So one morning after the crop was completed, I said to my father, "Father, I think we had better tell our negroes they are free and have a right to go where they please." He agreed it was the course to take, and we called them up and told them of their right to go or remain as they might choose, and that they were as free as we were, and I think we might have added, a little freer. And I assure you that the white women had the cooking to do that day, and many women who had never made a biscuit or fried ham and eggs, were forced to look into cook books to learn that which seemed to have come to the old black mammy by instinct.

But I want to tell you it did not take a lifetime for the poor ignorant negroes to learn the extent of their freedom and their rights thereunder. When they ascertained the fact that they had a right to stand and listen to a white man talk, and none dare molest or make them afraid, they took advantage of every opportunity to listen and to learn. And when the reconstruction measures were passed by Congress,[1] they were not long in learning that the bottom rail was on top. I remember and shall never forget the wonderful influence any worthless carpetbagger had on them to the exclusion of all advice any of us might give. Some irresponsible fellow put it into their heads that every slave was to be given forty acres of land and a mule from the lands of the former slave owners, and having once taken root, it spread through the land of the South, and was generally believed.

Once upon a time one of these slick friends of the former slaves, and who had such wonderful influence over them, taking advantage of the ignorance and confidence of an old time darkey, meeting him on his former master's plantation, informing the old ex-slave that he was one of the men whom the government had appointed to measure off the aforesaid forty acres and give him a deed to it, and that another man would be round soon to assign and deliver him his mule with which to work it. So with glad heart and ready hand the old negro assisted the pretended official in making the measurement. When that was done, the old man wanted his deed, which was readily written and delivered on the payment to the swindler of $8.75, being all the money the old man had. Some days after this the old negro seemed more independent than usual, and began putting on airs of ownership when his former master said to him, "Dick, what's the matter with you? For some time you have been putting on airs like you owned the place." "Yes, sar, I does own part of de place." "How's that? What do you mean, you old fool?" "Well, sar, de guberment man jist comed round and measured me off my forty acres offen your land, and gived me a deed to it." Much astonished, but knowing some fraud had been practiced upon the old darkey, the owner asked to see the deed. Thereupon the old man handed out his supposed deed for the inspection of his former master, and the present landlord, and when held up to the light of intelligence, the old man was dumbfounded to hear the words read, "As Moses lifted up the serpent in the wilderness, so have I lifted this old darkey out of eight dollars and seventy-five cents. Selah!" It was said long, long time ago that "a fool and his money are soon parted," and this is especially true where gross ignorance and unbounded confidence on one side and unscrupulousness on the other. But I have thought of all the villains known to mankind it is he who abuses the confidence reposed in him, and swindles under the guise of friendship. It puts me more in mind of the kiss with which our Saviour was betrayed than any with which I can compare it.

It was some years before the old darkey ceased saying, "Masser" when addressing a white man. Old Uncle Jim Hussey, a fine old time darkey, who lived and died near Mooresville in Lee county,

Mississippi, kept up the habit of calling his old friends Masser till the time of his death. There was another peculiarity about Uncle Jim which I do not think applies to any other ex-slave in all this country, and that is that he always under all circumstances voted the Democratic ticket. In the darkest days of Mississippi, when the colored population marched to the polls in solid phalanx and voted in columns for the Republican party, Uncle Jim always from the very beginning and as long as he voted, put in his vote for the Democrats. He always said that as the colored people were living with the whites and largely dependent upon them, it did seem to him that what was to the interest of one race must be equally so for the other, and that as the white people were the more intelligent, it stood to reason that they would advocate and vote for those principles which would make for their betterment and consequently for the best interests of all.

He was a fine old character, as polite as a Chesterfield, and as kind hearted as any man I have ever met, white or black. He thought nothing of taking off his hat and bowing graciously to anyone whom he met from pure politeness. But those kind are becoming fewer and fewer every year. If we had more such men as Uncle Jim, and fewer of the worthless and law-breaking class, the country would be better off.

December 7, 1906

Just what was heaped upon a proud and noble people here in the South after the war, none will ever know after this generation passes off the stage of action. We cannot write so succeeding generations can appreciate what we endured. The truth is that the South was settled by the chevaliers of England and their descendants, a proud and loyal people. In addition to this, they raised up what their enemies call a slave aristocracy, but which we thought of as agricultural kings, who lived on their plantations, surrounded by their slaves, managed generally by overseers, and dispensed hospitality like princes. Then we had the smaller slave-holders, nestled here and there amid these greater slave owners, and hoping to be larger owners of both slaves and land in the future, the most of those who did not own slaves hoped to do so some time in the future. There were really few of them of the renting class who aspired to no better situation in the financial world. The master owned his slaves, and when he said to one, "go," he went, and when he said to another, "do this," he did it. No questions were asked, but unquestioning obedience was the rule of the master. Not only this, but even those who did not own slaves, felt no hesitance in commanding them when about them as if they did own them. But when the reconstruction measures were enforced, all these ex-slaves were allowed to vote and hold office, while all the whites who had held any office, civil or military, in the United States, or in the different states, were disfranchised. As a general thing it was the custom to elevate to office our most intelligent and accomplished men; and so take the number who had held office, from the old men of eighty and the young men of twenty-one and all the way between, and there was a mighty host of our best men who could neither vote nor hold office under these infamous measures. Consequently, the negroes, just from the plow and the hoe, and having no learning, and in most instances no intelligence, took the offices and went to the capitals, to make laws for us. If a man is in bondage and has no desire for freedom and liberty of action and no aspirations for higher and loftier things, he may not suffer much from his condition, and especially when he has a kind and considerate master. But a proud, noble and intelligent people, like those of the South, to be subjected to such treatment as we received just after the war, was enough to cause more suffering and did cause more suffering than our slaves ever endured, mental suffering being so much worse than bodily suffering.

I myself was in Jackson, Mississippi when the legislature was in session during the seventies, and while there were not as many negroes then in the legislature as there had been, they very largely predominated. The Legislative Hall looked like a great dark cloud with a small white rift at the edge of it. You know I suggested some time back that it was quite probable that the negroes, just after the war, and before they were actually told by their owners that they might go free, had many whispered talks as to what the war would bring to them, being still under fear of their old owners.

The people of the South had seen much of sorrow and death

during the war, and had been beaten and overpowered by numbers and forced to submit. Her brave and chivalrous sons were resting beneath the soil of the many battlefields on which they had sustained Her honor, or their bones were bleaching Her plains, where no friendly eye ever saw their forms after they fell. The military power of the United States, dotting town and hamlet, held the survivors in subjection. We were thus held beneath the rod and afraid to make a move for our release. You can understand, when you are told that many men came down from the North to lead these ignorant slaves and fatten on the South, why the Jews so much hated one of their own race who became a tax collector under the Roman Empire, to whom they were subjected in the time of our Saviour's sojourn on earth. Men will have to be different to what they now are before they can quietly and placidly see their enemies take their sustenance, make the laws by which they are to be governed and appoint over them their former slaves to execute such laws. Nothing restrained our· people during those reconstruction days but the fear of the military power.

I remember very well how intense the feeling was against one, Flood, who was chief of the Registration Board at Fulton, where I then lived. That always was a white county, and it was almost impossible to restrain the boys from doing him some personal injury. He was a shrewd, unscrupulous adventurer, who came here, not to serve his country, but himself, and who ingratiated into the confidence of the negroes, and but for the fact that he feared the consequences of his conduct, would have remained there to try for office. But when the election was over by which the military constitution was adopted, he had seen enough to indicate to him that he might do better somewhere else. During the first campaign for the adoption or rejection of the constitution, which had been submitted to the people for ratification or rejection, I took a part in the speech making in opposition to the adoption. There were several features of that constitution which were so objectionable, that it failed of the necessary vote.[1] Then the military authorities, who were in charge of the entire South, and who had all power, eliminated certain of those objectionable features, and the constitution for Mississippi was again submitted, with those features left off, and thus carried.

In that first campaign Eugene Whitfield ran for Congress on the Republican ticket, and was opposed by a little fellow from the North, who ran for the same office, but now opposed the adoption of the constitution, and whom I suspect was here after the "loaves and fishes," as well as Flood. His name has passed out of my mind. I remember to have made a speech at old Ryan's Wells, north of Fulton, during this campaign, and in which Whitfield and his opponent also spoke. There was a yankee driving Whitfield around over the campaign, against whom Whitfield's opponent seemed to have great feeling for some cause, and when he rose to make his speech in opposition to the constitution and Whitfield, I saw him place a cocked pistol in his hat behind where he stood to make his address, and I thought sure he was going to open in warm style on Whitfield. But when he began he said, "Gentlemen, I am not after Colonel Whitfield. He is a nice gentleman. But I am after his carriage driver." And from that he went for the carriage driver in the roughest manner I have ever heard anyone abused from the stump, but he opened not his mouth. It seems he was a Republican booster of Whitfield, and was carrying him through the campaign.

When we had defeated the first constitution, we really did not know whether to be sorry or glad. Those were perilous times, and we knew not what a day might bring forth. So while we were sure we had right yet, fearing what might be the next move of the powers at Washington, we were ill at loss. But it came out all right, and this is another illustration of the doctrine, "Do right and leave the consequences to God."

December 14, 1906

Many of us remember and will ne'r forget the days from 1865 to 1875, ten eventful years in the history of our Southland. Of course it is impossible to paint in true colors the events of those years. Being under military rule part of the time, and under military power all this time, which means the same thing as military rule practically, we could do nothing openly that would alleviate our condition. What we did in the way of relief measures had to be done on the sly. Young men were growing up who had never been in the war, but whose hands were itching to take hold of something by which they might signalize their entrance into life's arena by some action for the benefit and relief of their country and which might put a feather in their own caps that would in some degree look like they were worthy sons of worthy sires; and so they were ever ready to do anything which might be thought to even tend toward relief, and doubtless would have been guilty of many indiscretions but for the advice of older and wiser heads. But in the meantime the negroes kept moving from bad to worse, led on by unworthy and often trifling white men. Under these circumstances many devices were resorted to to checkmate their political moves. An old friend of mine, just before an election, happened to come into the possession of a Republican ticket. He showed it to some of the Democratic leaders in an adjoining county and they were delighted to get it, saying it was the very thing they had been endeavoring to secure for some time. You see, before the Democrats came into power and passed a law that no picture or device of any kind should be printed on any ballot by which it could be distinguished and that all ballots should be alike, the ignorant negroes knew their Republican ticket by the picture that headed it, and not by the names which were written thereon. You see how easy it was for the "leading politicians" on our side to duplicate the ticket, how easily these bogus tickets could be placed in the hands of the ignorant voters and how the count would show up on our side. Again, men did not scruple to take out the votes which were actually cast and substitute the Democratic ticket therefor, and ease their conscience by the thought that "all things are fair in war," and that the good of the country demanded this. Sometimes one means was used and sometimes others to accomplish such action. It was well known that the most of the leaders of the negroes, both white and black, were quite venal and ready for a bid in money to betray their party. By this means the ignorant voter was often deceived by his pretended friends, and made really to vote the Democratic ticket, when he thought he was voting for the other side. Sometimes the tickets were exchanged by the art of legerdemain, so to speak, and the innocent leader gave out the tickets which had been left in place of the genuine article. You see the picture was there all the same, and it was that by which they³ judged. But, after a few of such tricks had been played on them, they were more careful and some other scheme had to be resorted to. The rule of the black voter was always to line up in solid column at voting time. This was very distasteful to the white man. Many means were resorted to to break up this custom. Sometimes the whites came to the polls with their cannons on the ground, booming them once and awhile while the white men stood 'round, and some of them occasionally fired off pistols or guns. There was nothing said to the negroes about not voting as they might please, and no intimidation whatever, but all the same the cannons were boomed and guns and pistols fired, and the negroes ran off and left the polls and never came back to vote.

Finally, in 1875, the whites decided they had had enough of it, and it must stop in some way. It was managed differently in different places. In Lee county we had a meeting of prominent workers for the cause and it was decided that everybody should be on a committee to make a general and close canvass of the county one day before the election and press home to the negroes every argument we could to induce them to vote with us. I remember very well to have been in that canvass. We searched out the brother in black and told them one by one in as much as we could, and each squad of whites numbering as many as we well could, and one man talking for awhile and then another. Many agreed to vote with us, but said it in such a way that we knew very well that they did not mean it. Many others were mum. On the next day when the polls were opened the whites were much and early on the ground, and when the negroes came in they did not present that solid black phalanx of column they had formerly done. The truth is they had been informed that it was not good manners. The most of them, though, were very anxious to vote the Republican ticket. No violence was offered, but many whites would surround a negro voter and use all kind of arguments and persuasions to vote the Democratic ticket, and as each voter could be induced to cast his vote in that way, the entire white contingent would raise a yell that would have done honor to the old Rebel soldier's battle cry; and thus one by one the negroes were induced to fall into line, except a few who retired to the rear without voting at all. This took place throughout the state, and the Republican party was put out of business in Mississippi.

NOTES

[1]The Congressional reconstruction acts of March 2 and 23, 1867, declared the "insurrectionary" states under military rule. The right of suffrage was conferred upon the freedmen and withheld from those who fought for or held sympathy for the Confederacy. Elections were later held to elect delegates to state conventions that would frame constitutions guaranteeing black political equality. The congressional program also required that before a state could be restored to the Union the new legislature must meet and ratify the 14th Amendment.

[2]The proposed Mississippi constitution of 1868 contained a number of features which white voters found objectionable, particularly a clause which barred from public office any individual who had fought for or aided the Confederacy. The constitution was defeated, and was revoted and passed in 1869 with many of the objectionable features removed.

[3]Black voters.

Epilogue

On December 14, 1906, Clayton closed his "Pen Pictures of the Olden Time." As he speaks across the years to us who have joined him in remembering the past, it is significant that he looks to the future. Though this collection has had to wait three-quarters of a century, perhaps it has come to a new set of "old and dear friends" at precisely the right time:

> And now these Pen Pictures close. They have given me considerable work, but have been a source of pleasure, too. Many people, young and old, here and elsewhere, have commended them very highly. Many people have asked me to have them published in book form. This would cost considerable labor and considerable money. Whether I shall do this sometime in the future depends upon health, and what demand may be made for such a book. And now I part from you all as old and dear friends part.
>
> > "To each, to all, a fair good night,
> > And airly dreams and slumbers light."

Index